TAKING BACK ISLAM

TAKING BACK ISLAM

American Muslims Reclaim Their Faith

Edited by Michael Wolfe
and the Producers of ⊚beliefnet

RODALE

© 2002 by Rodale Inc. and Beliefnet, Inc.
Cover Photo © by PhotoDisc

Printed in the United States of America
Rodale Inc. makes every effort to use acid-free ∞, recycled paper ♲.
Book design by Joanna Williams

Library of Congress Cataloging-in-Publication Data
    Taking back Islam : American Muslims reclaim their faith / [edited] by Michael Wolfe and the producers of Beliefnet.
        p.   cm.
    ISBN 1–57954–655–2   hardcover
    1. Islam—Essence, genius, nature.   2. Religious awakening—Islam.
    3. Islamic renewal.   4. Muslims—United States.   I. Wolfe, Michael,
    date.   II. Beliefnet (Firm)
    BP161.3 .T35   2002
    297'.0973—dc21   2002011081

Distributed to the book trade by St. Martin's Press

2   4   6   8   10   9   7   5   3   1   hardcover

Visit us on the Web at www.rodalestore.com, or call us toll-free at (800) 848-4735.

Visit Beliefnet on the Web at www.beliefnet.com.

WE **INSPIRE** AND **ENABLE** PEOPLE TO IMPROVE
THEIR LIVES AND THE WORLD AROUND THEM

ACKNOWLEDGMENTS

This collection is the result of heartfelt efforts by generous contributors across the country and beyond it. Many authors selflessly agreed to have their work tailored to the demands of the present volume, and often-difficult decisions were accepted with great grace at the last minute. Deborah Caldwell, Beliefnet's senior religion producer, deserves special thanks for her superb editing and her extensive and long-nurtured involvement with the Muslim writing community. In addition, the sustained efforts of Wendy Schuman, Elizabeth Sams, and Steve Waldman at Beliefnet as well as Troy Juliar, Stephanie Tade, and Jennifer Kushnier at Rodale Books, brought this book into being. Thanks to all for helping these voices to be heard.

—Michael Wolfe

CREDITS

CONTENTS

WHY NOW?
AN INTRODUCTION

By Michael Wolfe

In the months after September 11, American Muslims heard
the familiar, high-pitched grating sounds of Islam being defined
for us by others. On television, from the Capitol, from the
pulpit, in the classroom, and worst of all on videotapes from
Osama bin Laden's caves, we listened to commentators, politicians,
scholars, and rich terrorists in exile tell us the "real meaning" of our
faith. We heard anti-American fanatics quote the Qur'an to justify
mass murder, and we heard anti-Muslim bigots quote it back—
both sides using bad translations and phrases out of context. And
most of what we heard we didn't like because it was not accurate.
Publicly, we tried to counter these distortions—on air, in meetings
at our mosques, through visits to churches and synagogues. Since
then, we have sought to replace them with a truer interpretation:
that Islam is a peaceful, progressive, inherently forgiving and compassionate religion. Anyone who believes otherwise misses the
core values of Islam.

Privately, in our mosques and in our homes—away from the
judging ears of the world—we began talking to each other with an
honesty born of urgency. Little by little we began to arrive at some
common ground. We knew something had to be done or our religion risked being tarnished, even corrupted. We talked about our
leadership—and how dissatisfied we were with aspects of it. We
talked about the role of women—and how the Islam practiced in
many lands abroad, lands to which we had looked for guidance,

failed to capture the egalitarian spirit of the Islam we knew. We talked about violence—and how painful it was to accept that Islam, a religion whose name means "self-surrender," had been pressed into service by militant causes so often that, in many Western minds, it has become synonymous with violence.

We not only talked about what had gone wrong, but about how things ought to be. We began to conceive, voice, and then, finally, put to paper ideas about how *we* want to define Islam in this century. In the year since September 11, American Muslims began to do something extraordinary. We began to take back Islam.

As Ali Minai, a professor at the University of Cincinnati, remarks in "A Time for Renewal," the "interpretation of Islam can no longer be left to the most regressive segment of Muslim society. Muslims who believe that their faith is compatible with progressive humanist ideals must express themselves—not as apologists of Islam to the West but as proponents of new possibilities for Muslims." This is what our best-known non-Muslim historian of Islam, Karen Armstrong, means when she asks "Is this really a case of a faith being hijacked? Not yet. Because in this case, the other people aboard—as it were—can take an effective stand against the moral nihilism of the terrorists."

Taking Back Islam records the latest chapter in a centuries-long conversation that non-Muslims may never have heard. For Islam is surprisingly undoctrinaire and open to discussion. And as doctrines go, Islam's is simple—broad enough that 1.5 billion people around the world can agree on it. Only three things are really required to be a Muslim: belief in God, knowledge of his message, and respect for the prophets from Abraham to Jesus to Muhammad. Beyond that, quite a lot is up for grabs.

Muslims in general don't like the word "reform," with its various English connotations. Yet, as Salam al-Marayati reminds us in "The Rising Voice of Moderate Muslims," a kindred word is found in the Qur'an. "In Arabic, it is called *islah* and is the root meaning of the word *maslahah*, which means 'the public interest.' Historically, Muslim intellectual leaders such as Farangi Mahall Wali Allah, Jamal al-Din al-Afghani, and Muhammad Abduh . . . have used reason to create revivalist movements." Wali Allah of India helped to reaffirm the use of reason in legal interpretation and "condemned the blind imitation of tradition. Al-Afghani challenged Muslims to think of Islam as consistent with reason and science. Abduh believed in educational reforms throughout Muslim society." There is plenty of precedent, then, in Muslim thought for bringing Islam into close accord with people's present needs. Since September 11, however, a lot of American Muslims have begun to look beyond these classic independent thinkers of the nineteenth and twentieth centuries to think and write on their own authority.

September 11 forced a reckoning of sorts, and it has led us to be more self-reliant. When any religion is new to a place, as Islam is new to America, the tendency to take one's cues from the Motherland is strong, wherever that Motherland is perceived to be. *And then there comes a moment to grow up.* For many American Muslims, that moment arrived in the weeks following September 11, when a substantial number grew disenchanted with the habit of looking abroad for leadership. The near extinction of Afghanistan at the hands of the Taliban, the abysmal state of education in Pakistan, the murderous mullahs of al-Qaeda misquoting the Qur'an on video, along with a host of other glaring moral failures, have led many American Muslims to suspect that Islam's "traditional lands" have less to teach us than they claim.

Ten years from now, this period may mark the time when American Muslims found their real voice. *Taking Back Islam* is a book by progressive, mostly American, Muslims—people who are in love with Islam, who are proud of Islam, and who are confident enough in its strength to believe that it can stand up to honest introspection. "Speak the truth," the Prophet Muhammad said, "even if it hurts you." A sometimes-painful struggle of a faith in search of its soul informs this book. There runs through its pages an anxiousness for the life of a faith we love. This anxiousness is creative, giving rise to new formulations and fresh answers, and to a strong desire to tap the best traditions of Islam.

Many of the essays here are not about politics, and that in itself is significant. As their authors reflect on how to reclaim Islam, they often turn not to questions of power, but to matters of faith and practice and tradition. As Leila Dabbagh writes in "Muhammad's Legacy for Women," "My ancestors faithfully practiced the five pillars of Islam without losing sight of the fundamental requirements of everyday civil and compassionate living." Her words sound a theme we hear often in these pages, of "getting back to basics," of recovering the sweetness inherent in a religion that has been seriously injured from within by extremists and demonized from without. The Prophet Muhammad once was asked, "What is religion?" He answered, "One's regard and conduct towards others." That is the sort of vision American Muslims are trying, God willing, to reclaim.

AMERICAN MUSLIMS' SPECIAL OBLIGATION

AN AMERICAN MUSLIM LEADER ASKS: WHO HAS THE GREATEST RESPONSIBILITY TO STOP VIOLENCE COMMITTED BY MUSLIMS IN THE NAME OF ISLAM?

By Ingrid Mattson

September 11 exacerbated a double-bind American Muslims have been feeling for some time. So often, it seems, we have to apologize for reprehensible actions committed by Muslims in the name of Islam. We tell other Americans, "People who do these things (oppression of women, persecution of religious minorities, terrorism) have distorted the 'true' Islam."

And so often we have to tell other Muslims throughout the world that America is not as bad as it appears. We say, "These policies (support for oppressive governments, enforcement of sanctions responsible for the deaths of almost one million Iraqi children, vetoing any criticism of Israel at the United Nations) contradict the 'true' values of America."

But frankly, American Muslims have generally been more critical of injustices committed by the American government than of injustices committed by Muslims. This has to change.

For several years prior to September 11, I spoke publicly in Muslim forums against the injustice of the Taliban. My criticism of

1

this self-styled Muslim regime was not always well-received. Some Muslims felt that public criticism of the Taliban harmed Muslim solidarity. Others questioned my motives, suggesting that I was more interested in serving a feminist agenda than an Islamic one. My answer to the apologists has always been: Who has the greatest duty to stop the oppression of Muslims committed by other Muslims in the name of Islam? The answer, obviously, is Muslims.

I had not previously spoken about suicide attacks committed by Muslims in the name of Islam. I did not avoid the subject; it simply did not cross my mind as a priority among the many issues I felt needed to be addressed. This was a gross oversight. I should have asked myself, "Who has the greatest duty to stop violence committed by Muslims against innocent non-Muslims in the name of Islam?" The answer, obviously, is Muslims.

American Muslims, in particular, have a great responsibility to speak out. The freedom, stability, and strong moral foundation of the United States are great blessings for all Americans, particularly for Muslims.

Moreover, we do not have cultural restrictions that Muslims in some other countries have. In America, Muslim women have found the support and freedom to reclaim their proper place in the life of their religious community. And Muslims have pushed and been allowed to democratize their governing bodies. Important decisions relating to theological and legal matters are increasingly made in mosques and Islamic organizations by elected boards or the collective membership.

But God has not blessed us with these things because we are better than the billions of humans who do not live in America. We do not deserve good health, stable families, safety, and freedom more than the millions of Muslims and non-Muslims throughout the world who are suffering from disease, poverty, and oppression. Muslims who live in America are being tested by God to see if we will be satisfied with a self-contained, self-serving Muslim community that resembles an Islamic town in the Epcot global village, or if we will use the many opportunities available to us to change the world for the better—beginning with an honest critical evaluation of our own flaws.

Because we have freedom and wealth, we have a special obligation to help those Muslims who do not—by speaking out against the abuses of Muslim "leaders" in other countries.

So let me state it clearly: I, as an American Muslim leader, denounce not only suicide bombers and the Taliban, but those leaders of other Muslim states who thwart democracy, repress women, use the Qur'an to justify un-Islamic behavior, and encourage violence. Alas, these views are not only the province of a small group of terrorists or dictators. Too many rank-and-file Muslims, in their isolation and pessimism, have come to hold these self-destructive views as well.

The problem is that other Muslims may not listen to us, no matter how loud our voices. American Muslim leaders will be heard only if they are recognized as authentic interpreters of Islam among the global community. This will be very difficult to achieve because our legitimacy in the Muslim world is intimately linked with American foreign policy. An understanding of some important developments in Islamic history and theology will clarify this apparently odd dependence.

ISLAM IS WITHOUT CENTRAL LEADERSHIP

According to Islamic doctrine, after the death of the Prophet Muhammad, no Muslim has the right to claim infallibility in interpreting the faith. There is no ordination, no clergy, no unquestioned authority. This does not mean that all opinions are equal, nor that everyone has the ability to interpret religious and legal doctrine. Solid scholarship and a deep understanding of the tradition are essential. But not all scholars are considered authoritative. Most Muslims will accept the opinions only of scholars who demonstrate that they are truly concerned about the welfare of or-

dinary people. People simply will not listen to scholars who seem
to be mostly interested in serving the interests of the government.

Throughout Muslim history, religious leaders who advocated
aggression against the state were usually marginalized. After all,
most Muslims did not want to be led into revolution—they simply
wanted their lives to be better. The most successful religious
leaders were those who, in addition to serving the spiritual needs
of the community, acted as intermediaries between the people and
state. There have been times, however, when hostile forces attacked or occupied Muslim lands—the Mongol invasions, the
Crusades, European colonialism, and the Soviet invasion of
Afghanistan. At those times, people needed revolutionary leaders;
those who were unable to unite the people against aggression were
irrelevant.

The question we need to ask is, At this point in history, what
do Muslims need to hear from their leaders? What voices will they
listen to?

It often seems that American Muslims are asked to choose
between uncritical support for rebels acting in the name of Islam
or uncritical support for any actions taken by the American government. Muslim extremists have divided the world into two
camps: those who oppose the oppression of the Muslim people
and those who aid in that oppression. President Bush has divided
the world into two camps: those who support terrorism and those
who fight terrorism.

Where does this leave American Muslim leaders who oppose
the oppression of the Muslim people but who also want to fight
terrorism? In the increasingly strident rhetoric of war, we may be
considered traitors by both sides.

Nevertheless, we must continue to speak. We have to speak
against oppressive interpretations of Islam and against emotional,
superficial, and violent apocalyptic depictions of a world divided.
And in our desire to show ourselves to be patriotic Americans, we
cannot suppress our criticisms of the United States when we have

them. We have to do this, not only because it is the right thing to do, but also because if we do not, the Muslim world will remain deaf to our arguments that peaceful change is possible and that revolt and ensuing lawlessness almost always cause the greatest harm to the people.

It is in the best interest of the United States that we be permitted to continue to speak. In many parts of the world, those who speak out against corruption and unfair government policies are jailed, tortured, and killed. In such circumstances, very few people—only those who are willing to risk losing their property, their families, their security, and their lives—will continue to speak out. Only the radicals will remain.

Ingrid Mattson is vice president of the Islamic Society of North America, the oldest American Muslim advocacy and education group, and professor of Islamic Studies and Christian-Muslim Relations at Hartford Seminary.

A TIME FOR RENEWAL

A PAKISTANI-BORN PROFESSOR ARGUES THAT THE INTERPRETATION
OF ISLAM CAN NO LONGER BE LEFT TO THE FAITH'S
MOST REGRESSIVE SEGMENTS.

By Ali Minai

In the aftermath of the terrorist attacks of September 11, it has become accepted wisdom that "everything has changed." Usually, this refers to such things as political alignments, economic policy, and civil rights. From the viewpoint of those professing the Islamic faith, however, the events of September 11 represent a crisis of identity as well as a turning point in the usual sense.

As Americans made sense of their sudden and terrible encounter with the reality of global conflict, their response spanned the spectrum from thoughtful understanding to reflex bigotry. Fortunately, the latter response has been limited to isolated cases, thanks primarily to the responsible approach taken by political leaders at all levels.

I heard numerous dark predictions of the coming "hard times" from Muslim friends who have lived in the United States for years and decades. I did not dismiss their fears as unreasonable, but I believed that they were premature and gave too little credit to the nature of the American ethos. Unlike Old World societies with centuries of cultural layering, American society is a dy-

namic—and rather chaotic—mixture of constantly changing attitudes. This dynamic aspect imbues it with a certain disorder—but
also with the potential for rapid intellectual evolution, leading to
almost total unpredictability. In the language of physics, one might
say that the system operates in a state of perpetual "criticality,"
where almost everything is always possible, and the magnitude of
consequences bears no necessary relation to the size of the cause.
It is precisely this notion that is captured in such phrases as "only
in America," "the land of opportunity," and "the American Dream."

I do not think that American Muslims will give up so easily
on the complexity of a society that produced Franklin, Jefferson,
Lincoln, Frederick Douglass, Susan B. Anthony, and Martin Luther
King Jr. It is a society manifestly open to fresh understanding and
demonstrably fickle in its commitment to old dogma. The key
point about the current crisis is not that "everything has changed,"
but that "anything is possible."

It is, therefore, with some optimism that I note the primary
response of America to the "Islamic" aspect of the current crisis: A
dramatic increase of interest in Islam. By all accounts, translations
of the Qur'an and books on Islam are flying off the shelves at
bookstores, and suburbanite baby boomers throughout the land
are receiving their first impressions of a faith that moves more
than a billion people on this Earth. The question is: What impres-
sion will they get?

In the year since September 11, it has become routine for
politicians and pundits to proclaim that Islam is a "religion of
peace." This is a welcome development, and it should do American
Muslims a lot of good to have the virtue of their religion proclaimed loudly by the opinion-makers of this country. It can also
do a lot of harm, however, if Islam's newfound prominence in the
American consciousness were to lead to ultimate disillusionment.
And the potential for this disillusionment exists not only due to
the work of authors unfriendly to Islam but also because of the
words and deeds of Muslims themselves. In this time of danger and

opportunity, it is imperative that the Muslims of America (and the West in general) not allow a superficial reading of their faith to become its default image. But before this can be done, Muslims need to take stock of their own attitudes.

Strictly speaking, it is no more correct to say that Islam is peaceful than to proclaim that it is violent. The texts and traditions on which any faith's practice is based are open to multiple interpretations, and, as these interpretations pile up over the course of history, it becomes almost impossible to assert the existence of a unique orthodoxy. A liberal humanist Muslim can find enough in the Islamic texts to justify a peaceful view of Islam—and this is being done with great fervor these days. A militant Muslim seeking sanction for violence, however, can also find plenty in the same sources to proclaim holy war on the world. Islam is no more inherently violent or peaceful than Catholicism, which, at various times, has found justification for both Torquemada and Mother Teresa in the same tradition. This is the complexity that must not be obscured by simplistic attempts to understand Islam, and Muslims must play a crucial role in this matter. To put it bluntly: It is time for a vocal and successful reformist movement within Islam, and Muslims living in the West are in the best position to lead it.

While most Muslims believe in a benign—even benevolent—faith, it is an unfortunate historical fact that those charged with religious leadership among Muslims have often veered toward more exclusivist and austere interpretations. This is a propensity long recognized within Muslim societies and is notably evident in the classical literary traditions of Persian and Urdu. Far from being revered figures, the arbiters of official piety—the cleric, the jurist, the preacher, the paragon of piety, and the enforcer of morality—have long been the subject of ridicule in the literatures of Iran and Muslim South Asia. That this attitude has persisted through centuries of changing social climate indicates that it is an essential part of the Muslim ethos in these regions—driven, in part, by the competing Gnostic (Sufi) tradition, which tends to be more inclusive.

The current Islamic synthesis, however, has acquired a distinctly orthodox aspect, both in response to and under the influence of Western modernity. This development has many historical antecedents: the policies of India's Mughal rulers, the encounter between Islam and colonists, the success of Zionism, and the emergence of Wahhabi Islam primarily in Saudi Arabia, among others.

The important point is that a rather regressive, static, and parochial version of Islam has become prevalent among the intelligentsia of the Muslim world. While this does not, in itself, generate militancy, it does provide sanction to exclusivist—and sometimes even bigoted—attitudes adopted by a small militant minority. In combination with the socioeconomic failure of almost all Muslim nations, this vision of Islam (which is partly responsible for the failure) has created a pervasive culture of grievance in the Muslim world. It is a culture that sees all problems afflicting Muslims as the result of a vast conspiracy—variously orchestrated by the "usual suspects": Jews, Christians, Hindus, ethnic Chinese, even Muslims of other sects. This culture takes real but mundane disputes over land, water, language, ethnicity, and oil and turns them into millennial confrontations.

In this apocalyptic worldview, Osama bin Laden makes perfect sense. Without changing this mindset, no amount of military action will rid the world of Islamic militants. The swamp that must be drained is not in the mountains of Afghanistan, but in the minds of hundreds of millions of Muslims. It is time for a new synthesis in Islam, and it can only be done from within by enlightened, informed, and faithful Muslims.

The crisis of September 11 has brought the Muslim world to a point of great opportunity. As the rest of the world discovers Islam, let it discover a progressive, enlightened, and dynamic faith suitable for the future, rather than an orthodoxy created by traditionalists still hankering for the past. All Muslims believe that the words of the Qur'an are eternal, but that is no excuse to freeze the process of their interpretation. If the words are to provide guidance in an ever-changing world, they must speak in ever-changing ways.

Once again, the sacred texts must be regarded as the source of principles rather than a prescription for piety. The famously closed door of interpretation must be reopened. Unfortunately, it is difficult to do this in most Muslim societies with traditional strictures, and previous attempts to do so have met with only limited success. A movement for true reform in Islamic thinking is more feasible in the West, with its guaranteed freedoms and its provision of space for new ideas.

The process must be a careful one, so as not to injure the basic precepts of the faith. It must be thoughtful, so that it does not antagonize believing Muslims. It must be based on rigorous scholarship, so that it carries weight. And it must be daring, so that it can inspire.

The interpretation of Islam can no longer be left to the most regressive segment of Muslim society. Muslims who believe that their faith is compatible with progressive humanist ideals must express themselves—not as apologists of Islam to the West but as proponents of new possibilities for Muslims.

Those who lament the fact that Islam today wears the face of militancy in the eyes of the world should keep this in mind: When those who are moderate do not speak as loudly as the militants, the militants speak for them too. The only way to reclaim the enlightened aspect of Islam is to pursue it aggressively. Call it extremism in the pursuit of moderation. And that is no vice.

Ali Minai was born in Karachi, Pakistan, and has lived in the United States since 1985. He is currently an associate professor in the Electrical & Computer Engineering and Computer Science Department at the University of Cincinnati, where his research focuses on the area of complex adaptive systems and distributed artificial intelligence. An avid student of history and politics, he writes in both English and Urdu.

HAS ISLAM BEEN HIJACKED?

THE BIOGRAPHER OF THE PROPHET MUHAMMAD AND AN EXPERT
ON FUNDAMENTALISM SAYS SEPTEMBER 11 IS A WATERSHED MOMENT
FOR ALL THE ABRAHAMIC FAITHS.

By Karen Armstrong

There has been much talk of the Islamic religion itself having been
"hijacked" by terrorists in the wake of September 11. The appalling
crime against humanity violated the cardinal principles of Islam
and has taken it off in quite the wrong direction. Certainly, this action seemed to endorse the mistaken view so common in the West
that Islam is essentially a fanatical and violent faith.

But is this really a case of a faith being hijacked? No, because
in this case, the other people aboard—as it were—can take an effective stand against the moral nihilism of the terrorists.

You'll recall that the primary meaning of the word jihad is
not "holy war" but "struggle" or "effort." This is a very important religious principle. It reminds us that religion is never something
achieved or finished. The revelation is given, but those who follow
it have to make a constant effort, day by day, year after year, to put
it into practice in a flawed and tragic world.

Each faith tradition represents a constant dialogue between
a timeless, transcendent, or sacred reality and the constantly
changing circumstances of life here on Earth. We all have to

struggle to make our scriptures and the insights of our tradition speak to the circumstances we find ourselves in.

These circumstances are always unique. The September 11 events gave Muslims a terrible insight into the way their faith can be abused and made an instrument of evil. Now they must initiate a new jihad, a new effort to delve creatively into their rich faith traditions and emphasize as never before the compassion, justice, and tolerance that are central to the Qur'anic vision.

All over the world, Muslim leaders and scholars have condemned the atrocity. But verbal declarations are not what religion is about. The struggle, or jihad, must continue in practical ways. Every time a violent action or an intolerant word is spoken, the world becomes a worse place, and the virus of hatred and evil spreads. But every time any single believer reaches out to others in compassion and sympathy, the world is improved infinitesimally. That daily, hourly effort is the jihad required right now.

Muslims don't carry this responsibility alone. Jews and Christians belong to the same religious family; they too can use this trauma creatively to reaffirm the values that we all hold in common. The religions of Abraham all worship the same God; all three have a deep commitment to compassion, justice, and peace.

We haven't always realized this. Christians have persecuted Jews relentlessly; they have led Crusades against Muslims. For centuries, Jews and Muslims lived together in peace in the Middle East, but for nearly one hundred years, they too have been locked in a terrible conflict, leading them to revile each other's religious traditions. This must stop. We have just had a terrible revelation about where such hatred can lead.

Religion, like any other human activity, can be abused. And the particular temptation of monotheism, with its personalized conception of the divine, has been to assume that God is a being like ourselves writ large, with likes and dislikes similar to our own. The Crusaders went into battle to slaughter Muslims with the cry, "God wills it!" I am pretty sure that the hijackers went to their deaths with much the same cry on their lips on September 11.

But obviously "God" wills nothing of the sort. What the Crusaders and the terrorists were doing was projecting their own hatred onto a Being they had created in their own image and likeness. God can all too easily be made to give a sacred seal of absolute approval to our most loathsome prejudices and policies. And now monotheists must be more careful of falling into this idolatry than ever before.

Far from being addicted to warfare, Islam insists on the importance of peace. The message of the Qur'an is a plural vision; it respects and values other traditions. When the Prophet Muhammad told the Muslim community that in the future they must pray facing Mecca (instead of Jerusalem, the Muslims' first orientation), he was trying to return to the time of Abraham, when, he imagined, believers didn't consider themselves Jews or Christians, did not argue about theological issues (such as the divinity of Christ) that nobody could prove one way or the other. They did not claim that their tradition had the monopoly on truth or that other ways of being religious were inferior, but were united in their faith.

In the early days of his mission, Muhammad seems to have assumed that Jews and Christians belonged to the same religion: After all, they all worshipped the same God. When, later, he found that in fact they had serious theological disagreements, he was shocked. It seemed perverse and wrong to him that people who surrendered their entire lives to God should quarrel with one another about abstruse theological matters—it was God that mattered, not how people interpreted their experience of the divine.

It was not that Muhammad thought that everybody should belong to one giant world religion. The Qur'anic view is that God has sent prophets to every people on the face of the Earth, who speak his word to them in their own languages and their own cultural traditions. The Qur'an was a scripture in Arabic for the Arabs, though anybody of any race was welcome to join. Muhammad never expected Jews or Christians to convert to Islam unless they specifically wished to do so because he believed they had received perfectly valid revelations of their own. But he also believed that they should stress the things that united them instead of exalting their own traditions at the expense of other faiths.

We need to cultivate this "Abrahamic" spirit during these terrible days. All of us—Jews, Christians, and Muslims—have used our religions to denigrate and even to persecute others. But Abraham is our common father, and if we can use September 11 to realize that we must not exalt our own faiths at the expense of others', perhaps something good can come out of evil.

If the atrocity is used by Christians and Jews to ostracize all Muslims and to denounce their faith as inherently evil, then it would not simply be Islam that was in danger of being hijacked on September 11, but Judaism and Christianity too.

British writer Karen Armstrong, a former Catholic nun, is the author of a celebrated, best-selling account of Christianity, Judaism, and Islam, A History of God, Islam: A Short History, Muhammad: A Biography of the Prophet, and The Battle for God, on fundamentalism in the major religions. She teaches at Leo Baeck College, a seminary for Reform Judaism in London.

THE MUSLIM VANGUARD

PROGRESSIVE ISLAMIC SCHOLAR FARID ESACK SAYS IT'S CRUCIAL
TO REVIVE THE VALUES OF COEXISTENCE AND TOLERANCE.

An Interview with Farid Esack by the editors of U.S. Catholic *magazine*

> *Islamic scholar Farid Esack has become one of the most sought-*
> *after interpreters of Islamic thought in the United States. A pro-*
> *gressive Muslim theologian from South Africa who cut his teeth*
> *in the anti-Apartheid struggle, Esack received his theological*
> *education in Pakistan. While studying in some of the same*
> *Karachi schools that also educated the leaders of the Taliban,*
> *he became increasingly disillusioned with both the narrow Is-*
> *lamic ideology and the oppression of Christians he encountered*
> *there. Pakistani Catholics introduced Esack to the ideas of lib-*
> *eration theology. He is the author of* On Being a Muslim *and*
> Qur'an: Liberation and Pluralism.

**In the U.S. media, you seem to have become the go-to guy for a
progressive voice of Islam. How large a movement is progressive
Islam?**

Like most religious movements, we claim we've always been there
and that there have always been strands of it in Islam. But progressive Islam has never been in the forefront, has never been the
accepted official theology. To be honest, we are a small minority in
different parts of the world, but the current crisis seems to be

pushing people into a greater understanding and appreciation of progressive Islamic theology.

What does progressive Islam offer in the current crisis?

We Muslims often argue about what the Prophet Muhammad did or didn't do, or about whether something was sanctioned by the Prophet or by early Muslims. Such theological precedents are very important to us.

Shortly after the bombing happened, as I was teaching a class and talking about Muhammad's life in Mecca and Medina, it occurred to me that it is a problem for us Muslims that we have only two theological paradigms and precedents on which to base our lives, and that that limitation is in part responsible for the mess that we are in. The one is the paradigm of a community of oppressed people in Mecca, and the other is of a Muslim community that is in control in Medina. What we don't have is a model for co-existing with other people in equality.

But there is a third way, what I call the Abyssinian paradigm, which refers to the time when the Prophet sent a group of his followers from Mecca to go and live in Abyssinia. They lived there peacefully for many years, and some of them did not return, even after Muslims were in power in Mecca. They did not make any attempts to turn Abyssinia into an Islamic state. They sent good reports back about the king under whom they were living and how happy they were living there.

This is the third paradigm that Muslims today more than ever need to revive because it is crucial for the sake of human survival and coexistence. Until recently, the notion of coexistence and cultural tolerance was pretty controversial for mainstream Islamic thinkers, but I was surprised at a recent Muslim conference to hear more and more people talking about the need to revive this Abyssinian paradigm. Mainstream Islam is beginning to listen to what we are saying.

What kind of responses do you see within the Muslim community in the aftermath of September 11?

I see mostly two responses, particularly within the Muslim community in the United States. The one asks, "How can we show people a different, better face of Islam?" The other one—and it's not the majority response—asks, "How can we radically transform the faith of Islam?" And for that agenda, it's incidental whether other people see a better face or not.

It is true that a significant part of the community has, quite frankly, secretly—and in some parts of the world, even openly— rejoiced in the attacks on the World Trade Center and the Pentagon. Another part of the Muslim world has been unequivocal in its condemnation and sadness about these events.

Then there are others who, while sad about the loss of innocent human lives, nevertheless would have had no issue with seeing those buildings go. For them, the buildings were symbolic of a different kind of "terrorism" represented by the global economic system and its effect on the Third World. As a direct result of the bombing of Afghanistan, that kind of resentment toward the United States has further increased.

Is that resentment widely shared in the Islamic world?

I don't think it is limited to the Islamic world. For example, after the 1991 Gulf War, Iraq's leader, Saddam Hussein, who sent thousands of Kurdish people to their deaths with chemical weapons, was voted Man of the Year by 94 percent of the African listeners of the BBC. I wouldn't be surprised at all if this year Osama bin Laden will emerge as Man of the Year in Africa.

Resentment of the U.S. is widespread across the Third World. On September 11, people in many black townships in South Africa were rejoicing, as were some in Latin America. But the news value of this rejoicing only extended to reactions in the Middle East.

So while it is not a peculiarly Muslim phenomenon, this re-

sentment does perhaps get aggravated in the Muslim world because for many Muslims, it's a double anger. It's both an anger at
the fact that the United States is controlling relations all over the
world and an anger at the fact that Muslims are not the ones in
control.

The particular Muslim resentment about not being the ones
in control stems from ancient memories of the first Medina, the
so-called Golden Age of Islam, and the desire to return to this state
of near-mythical perfection. Medina is seen as the perfect paradise
on Earth, as a time when Muslims ruled the world and everything
about it is glorified and mythologized.

This mythical period is contrasted with the misery of today.
The current image of the Muslim world is one of ruin and devastation, petty dictatorships and wars, starvation and begging bowls,
and an endless current of refugees. So when you can't gel your
glamorized version of your past with your current reality, it leads
to a pretty messed-up psyche.

**How large a role does the U.S. alliance with Israel play in driving
the resentment of the United States in the Muslim community?**

U.S. foreign policy on Israel is certainly a key factor. If one leaves
aside the notion of God as a real estate agent, today's Israel is
viewed as a colonialist implant in the Middle East. Its policies, particularly in the occupied territories, have created enormous resentment and bitterness. U.S. support for Israel is held up as the
example par excellence of the hypocrisy of U.S. foreign policy.

I believe in the right of Israel to exist. We have to accept reality because too much water has flowed under the bridge.

**The United States armed Saddam to fight the Iranians; we armed
the predecessors of the Taliban to fight the Soviets; now we're getting into bed with the Northern Alliance. Is the U.S. realpolitik approach to foreign policy contributing to our problems in the
Middle East?**

Absolutely. Much of what we have seen these days is really the comeuppance of earlier policies. The chickens are coming home to roost. But I don't think the United States has learned its lessons in terms of the allies it takes on board.

Now the U.S. government acts out of great anger. There is a kind of cowboy mentality that has set in. Nobody wants to think, and then people come and ask me, "Okay, so tell us: What do you think we should be doing now?" That question is very narrowly focused on what we should do now in response to what has just happened and whether there is any alternative to bombing.

People don't want to discuss things in long terms; they don't want to look at the broader picture. It doesn't fit into a sound bite. If it takes longer than a minute, then we don't have the time.

So now that we are in the middle of a war, is it too late to come up with constructive solutions?

Unfortunately, we know, and the government knows, that these terrorist networks are all over the world. They are very diffuse. In moments of anger, it's understandable to act a bit silly and to imagine that you're going to wipe out terrorism once and for all. But look, for example, at Britain and the Irish question, or Spain and the Basque problem. These problems have been running for decades and decades.

At the end of the day, there has to be an acknowledgment that there were grievances underneath all of these conflicts and that there is no way we will ever be able to sleep peacefully unless we begin to address these grievances.

Is the current crisis an isolated conflict with Islamic fundamentalists, or is this part of a broader conflict between the West and the Islamic world?

I see it as a clash between two religious fundamentalisms. On the one side, you have the Taliban, Osama bin Laden, al-Qaeda, and the actions we have witnessed. All that clearly represents the fanaticism of a religious fundamentalism.

On the other side of the conflict, we are dealing with another religious fundamentalism, one that is not generally recognized as such. The Buddhist theologian David Loy has described faith in the free market as a religion, a religion with a transcendent god, a god that is worshiped and that its adherents have a deep yearning to embrace and to be at one with—and that god is capital.

It also has a theology in the form of economics, a fundamentalist ideology that excludes all others. Its cathedrals are the shopping malls, and there is paradise or the promise of paradise for those who get on board. It is the fastest growing religion in the world today.

If you look at the language of President Bush, his notion of absolute evil and complete abhorrence, as well as Osama's language of complete abhorrence, neither recognizes the possibility of any grace on the other side. Both espouse very hardened kinds of fundamentalisms.

I don't think that Bush is the problem, but neither is Osama solely the problem. It's these fundamentalisms and what gives rise to them that are the crucial issue.

You've had a lot of contact with Islamic fundamentalists. How do you talk with them?

Sometimes I'm a bit adventurous. I recently went to a conference in Michigan of a very conservative Muslim group that had its origins in the broader Islamic fundamentalist movement. I expected to be walking into the lion's den, but instead I found that many people from this group were actually happy to see me and talk to me. It takes some courage to actually go and engage people, but we don't have an alternative to it.

I really believe that fundamentalism is a mindset. I'm currently teaching at Union Theological Seminary in New York, and there are a good number of "fundamentalists" here. Fundamentalism can be economic, or it can be feminist. There are all sorts of fundamentalisms.

The fundamentalist mindset comes from insecurities and fears, and if you want to engage fundamentalists, you need to learn how to address these fears. It is a struggle that needs to be fought at personal, educational, and political levels.

But how could our political and cultural tension escalate to such awful terror acts?

You have to try to think this through from a different point of view. We don't have any problem understanding how the passengers of the flight that crashed in Pennsylvania lunged to the cockpit to get to these hijackers. But they knew their actions meant that they were going to die in the process. The sure prospect of their own deaths didn't keep them from doing what they had to do to prevent greater harm, essentially to save a larger part of humankind.

Difficult as this may be for us to understand, in the twisted minds of these suicide bombers, they too saw themselves as giving their lives so that a larger part of humanity may live. For them, the United States is the enemy, Satan incarnate, who is causing chaos and destruction around the world.

How does the history of the Christian-Muslim encounter over the centuries continue to play into current conflicts?

Both of us—Muslims and Christians—haven't learned adequately how to confront our histories. Muslim-Christian tensions continue to play a very important role. If you look at Kosovo, at Bosnia, at Chechnya, it's amazing the kind of incidents and anecdotes that people invoke. People speak about massacres of four hundred or five hundred years ago as if they happened yesterday. The memory of the past is still very much with us.

What should people know about the history of Christian-Muslim relations?

Certainly the importance of the Crusades. When President Bush talked about launching a "crusade" against terrorism, he apparently didn't know that was a bad choice of words. It's true that the word "crusade" has many other uses in the English language today—people talk about a crusade against guns or a crusade against immorality. But because of the history of the medieval Crusades, this word represents coded language for Muslims.

Of course, history also frequently is manipulated. For example, Jerusalem has only become as important as it is in today's Muslim imagination over the past fifty years. And that happened as a result of political tensions and interests. Today Jerusalem looms far larger in the Muslim religious imagination than it has ever before.

What can ordinary people do to help Christian-Muslim relations?

People need to begin to deepen their encounters with others. Interfaith dialogues are a good place to start.

It's true that sometimes they can seem like somewhat irrelevant forums for a polite show-and-tell. You meet with these other nice people and show them your religion's nice verses about peace and justice and living in harmony, and then you get a nice pat on your back from the other people in the interfaith forum: "Good boy, good boy."

In my book *Qur'an: Liberation and Pluralism*, I took a different approach, looking not at the "nice verses" but rather at the difficult texts of the Qur'an.

I was reminded of that by a letter in the *New York Times* from someone who was upset about hearing that an imam had said that the Jews and the Christians will never be happy with you until you abandon your religion. She was upset with the imam, but the article she was referring to didn't mention that the imam's quote was actually from the Qur'an. Those kinds of things don't usually get dealt with when dialogue is stuck in politeness. As someone once put it, "Is there life after tea?"

But despite such limitations, by the end of the day, we don't have an alternative to engaging in conversation. The world we live in today is completely intertwined. You can't unbake the cake of globalization. You can't separate the sugar from the flour from the water from the vanilla from the cream. What you do to Muslims in the world today, you do to Christians; what you do to straight people, you do to gay people; and what you do to black people, you do to white people. The essential condition of humanness today is interconnectedness.

How do you teach or promote this sense of interconnectedness and tolerance?

I think we need to move more consciously toward a new kind of internationalization that is based on what ordinary people have in common with each other, not on the interests of the elites. Instead of talking about the global reach of the Internet or fast food or fashions, this new internationalization concerns itself with the ties that link the struggles of farmers in Colombia, for example, with the farmers in the Philippines.

Religious people, of course, have always been at the cutting edge of this kind of universalization, in part because we've always believed that our messages were universal. At the same time we need to acknowledge that this also has a downside when we couch our universal religious messages in superiority.

What's the particular role of the United States in today's interconnected world?

I think most people here don't have a very accurate perception of their country's role and relations in the world. I sometimes think of the United States as a very large house that has a huge extended family living in it. The house is headed by the big brother. Every day he comes home with chocolates and sweets, and he looks after the family very, very well.

This family never actually leaves the house. So they have no idea where big brother gets all his goodies from, and they're not very interested in finding out either. They're only too grateful that he's sharing them. They have no idea that, with the help of other bullies in the neighborhood, big brother has been throwing stones and creating havoc all around the block and in other neighborhoods as well.

Then one day, somebody throws a huge brick into the house and hurts several of the family's little sisters and brothers. The family is both angry and confused because big brother has been regaling them with stories about how nice he has been to everybody in the world and how many sweets he has been dishing out to so-and-so. And now so-and-so has come and thrown this brick at the house and hurt the little kids.

So everyone is just completely puzzled at why anyone in the world would do something like that. But big brother quickly says, "It's just because they're jealous of me. They're not built as well and not as good-looking as I am."

Perhaps the challenge for the U.S. is to become less great—if you insist on defining greatness in terms of "well-having." I think the measure of greatness should instead be on "well-being." In the meantime, it would be wonderful if the U.S. could exercise its greatness with more humility.

VIOLENCE

Nothing in the Qur'an or Muhammad's example justifies the attacks of September 11, though the perpetrators themselves, employing narrow, self-serving readings, would like the world to think otherwise.

The Qur'an specifically outlaws both suicide and wholesale reprisals against noncombatants. As Dr. Khaled Abou El Fadl writes in his essay "Peaceful Jihad," terrorism, *fasad fi al-'ard* in the Qur'an, is in effect to "wage war against God by dismantling the very fabric of existence." Even in a legitimate war, Muslims are required only to "go as far as it takes to stop aggression," notes Imam Yahya Hindi, elucidating passages in the Qur'an that define the permissible rules of engagement. "You get someone out of your home, you don't shoot him after he is out . . . the idea is that justice prevails."

Clearly, all this is a long way from the activities of al-Qaeda, the bombing of embassies, and the blowing up of airplanes and office buildings. And that is the point. These are only a few of the many Islamic precepts that the boys with their bombs and broken-down scholarship fail to cite in self-serving manifestos.

Americans of other faiths should know that American Muslims lamented and continue to lament the events of September 11. Who would be pleased to have their religion claimed by a group of murderously suicidal hijackers? In the longer run, too, there is a whole vocabulary of violence from which Islam needs to shake free. A challenge for American Muslims, as Dr. El Fadl writes, is how to reverse the way in which "political interests have come to dominate the public discourse, and to a large extent, moral discourses have become marginalized in modern Islam." Or one might say, extremists and political theorists have been stealing the show here.

Taking Back Islam has many meanings. Certainly one is to restate the fact that *how you act* determines the value of your action, and action beyond the moral pale has no worth whatever. As Aasma Khan notes in her essay on the efforts of young American Muslims to combat terrorism and violence, "By confronting intolerance and hatred, we delegitimize the message sent by terrorist attacks. Instead, we must stand for justice, even if it is against ourselves (Qur'an 4:135). When we achieve justice for all—women, men, black, white, yellow, brown, red, Muslim, non-Muslim—we make it possible to forge a lasting peace."

There are plenty of eloquent precedents in Western culture that demonstrate the inherent failures of terrorism. Just as Americans of other faiths need to understand more about Islam, so Muslims need to become more familiar with Western culture and its literature. Shakespeare, near the end of his play *King John* speaks succinctly:

> *There is no sure foundation set on blood,*
> *No certain life achieved by others' death.*

IS ISLAM VIOLENT?

A NOTED HISTORIAN ASKS, "WHAT RESPONSIBILITY DOES ISLAM BEAR
FOR SUICIDE BOMBERS AND OTHER ACTS OF VIOLENCE?"

By Karen Armstrong

The word Islam, which means submission to the will of God, is related to the Arabic *salam*, peace. When the Prophet Muhammad brought the revealed scripture called the Qur'an ("recitation") to the Arabs in the early seventh century C.E., one of his main purposes was precisely to stop the kind of indiscriminate killing we saw on September 11.

At the time, the Arabian Peninsula was in crisis. The tribal system was breaking down, and the various tribes were locked into a murderous cycle of vendetta and countervendetta. For a weak tribe, or a man who lacked powerful protection, survival was nearly impossible. The Prophet himself suffered several assassination attempts, and when his religious and social message ran him afoul of the establishment of Mecca, the small Muslim community was persecuted. Things got so bad that the Muslims had to migrate to Medina, some 250 miles to the north, and there they were subject to attack by the Meccan army, the greatest power in Arabia.

For about five years, there was war, and the Muslims narrowly escaped extermination. Terrible things were done on both sides. But when Muhammad sensed that the tide had just begun to turn in his favor, he completely changed tack. He concentrated on building a peaceful coalition of tribes and initiated an inspired, brave, and ingenious policy of nonviolence. This proved so successful that eventually Mecca voluntarily opened its gates to the Muslims, without bloodshed.

WAR ENDANGERED EARLY MUSLIMS

Because the Qur'an was revealed in the context of an all-out war, several passages deal with the conduct of armed conflict. Warfare was a desperate business in Arabia. An Arab chieftain was not expected to take prisoners; it was a given that he would simply kill everybody he could get his hands on. Muhammad knew that if the Muslims were defeated, they would all be slaughtered to the last man or woman.

Sometimes the Qur'an seems to have imbibed this spirit. Muslims are ordered by God to "slay [the enemy] wherever you find them" (4:89). Muslim extremists like bin Laden like to quote these verses, but they do so selectively, never quoting the exhortations to peace and forbearance that in almost every case mitigate these ferocious injunctions in the verses immediately following. Thus, "If they leave you alone and offer to make peace with you, God does not allow you to harm them" (4:90).

The only war condoned by the Qur'an, therefore, is a war of self-defense. "Warfare is an awesome evil" (2:217), but sometimes it is necessary to fight in order to bring the kind of persecution suffered by the Muslims to an end (2:217) or to preserve decent values (22:40). But Muslims may never initiate hostilities, and aggression is forbidden by God (2:190). While the fighting continues, Muslims must dedicate themselves wholly to the war in order to bring things back to normal as quickly as possible, but the second the enemy sues for peace, hostilities must cease (2:192).

The word jihad is much misunderstood. It is rarely used as a noun in the Qur'an, but in a verbal form, meaning "striving, struggle, or effort." This jihad denotes the determined effort that Muslims must make to put God's commands into practice in a terrible and evil world. Sometimes this will mean armed struggle, but the jihad also refers to a spiritual, moral, intellectual, social, domestic, or purely personal effort. There is a very famous and much-quoted *hadith* or traditional saying about the Prophet Muhammad, which describes him returning home after a battle and saying to his companions: "We are returning from the Lesser Jihad [the battle] to the Greater Jihad," which is the far more important and urgent struggle to reform one's own heart and one's own society.

Consequently, the Qur'an is quite clear that warfare is not the best way of dealing with difficulties. It is much better to sit down and reason with people who disagree with us and to "argue [with unbelievers] in the most kindly manner, with wisdom and goodly exhortation." If Muslims are forced to respond to an attack, their retaliation must be appropriate and proportionate to the wrong suffered, but forbearance is preferable: "To bear yourselves with patience is far better for you, since God is with those who are patient in adversity" (16:125–27).

The Qur'an also echoes the Jewish Torah, which permits the *lex talionis*—an eye for an eye and a tooth for a tooth—but adds that it is a meritorious act to be charitable and to refrain from retaliation (5:45).

ISLAM ALLOWS DIFFERENCE, INSISTS ON TOLERANCE

Muslims must be realistic. If God had wanted all peoples to be the same and have identical opinions and policies, then he would have made them into one nation and made them all Muslims. But God has not chosen to do this, so Muslims must accept his will (10:99; 11:118). If there is an irreconcilable difference, Muslims must simply go their own way, as the Prophet himself did when he found that he could not agree with the Meccan establishment, saying, "Unto you your moral law, and unto me, mine" (109:6). You go your way, and I'll go mine.

Above all, "There must be no coercion in matters of faith" (2:256). The grammar here is very strong, very absolute (*La ikra fi'l-din*). It is similar in form to the *shahada*, the Muslim profession of Faith: "There is no God but Allah!" (*"La illaha ill Allah!"*). The Unity of God is the basis of all Muslim morality and spirituality. The principle of *tawhid* (unity, oneness) is the Muslim task par excellence. Nothing must rival God—no ideology, material goods, or personal ambitions. A Muslim must try to integrate his entire personality and his whole life to ensure that God is his top priority, and in the unity that he will discover within himself when this is achieved, he will have intimations of that Unity which is God. It is, therefore, significant that in the Qur'an, the prohibition of force and compulsion in religious matters is made as emphatically as the assertion of the Unity of God. The principle is as sacred as that.

Muhammad did not intend to found a new world religion to which everybody had to subscribe. The Qur'an makes it clear that he considered that he was simply bringing the religion of the One God to the Arabs, who had not had a prophet before and had no scriptures in their own language. The Qur'an insists that its revelation does not cancel out the revelations made to previous prophets: to Abraham, Moses, David, Solomon, Enoch, or Jesus. Every nation on the face of the Earth has been sent some kind of revelation, which it expresses in its own cultural idiom. So every rightly guided religion comes from God.

In the Qur'an, Muslims are commanded to speak with great courtesy to Jews and Christians, "the People of the Book," who believe in the same God as they do (29:46). These were the world faiths that Muslims were familiar with. Today, Muslim scholars argue that had the Prophet known about Buddhists, Hindus, the Native Americans, or Australian Aborigines, the Qur'an would have endorsed their religious leaders too. Muhammad simply thought that he was bringing the Arabs, who seemed to have been left out of the divine plan, into the religious family founded by the other great prophets.

This is reflected in the symbolic story of the Prophet's spiritual flight from Mecca to Jerusalem, where he is welcomed by all the great prophets of the past on the Temple Mount, preaches to them there, and then ascends to the Divine Throne, greeting and sometimes taking advice from Moses, Aaron, Jesus, John the Baptist, and Abraham on the way. It is a story of religious pluralism: The prophets all affirm one another's visions and teachings; they gain help from one another. And it also shows the Prophet's yearning to bring the Arabs in far-off Arabia into the heart of the monotheistic faith.

So when Osama bin Laden declared a jihad against Christians and Jews, he was acting against basic tenets of the Qur'an. It goes without saying that any form of indiscriminate "killing" (qital), which is strongly condemned in the Qur'an, is also un-Islamic.

So too is suicide, which is forbidden in Islamic law. True, the Qur'an promises that those who fall in battle while fighting for their lives against Mecca will surely go to Paradise. It was certainly not encouraging Muslims to rush out and expose themselves to the danger of certain death.

It is perhaps important to note that suicide bombers are not simply trying to achieve a first-class ticket to heaven, as Westerners sometimes imagine. The Greek word from which we derive our "martyr" means witness. So does the Arabic for martyr: shahīd. When Christians were being persecuted by the Roman Empire, they believed that in their deaths they were witnessing to values that were higher than those of the coercive, persecuting state. It was a way of giving dignity and meaning to their terrible deaths.

Muslims have the same ideal. They all honor the Prophet's grandson, Husain, a special hero of Shi'ite Muslims. Husain and his band of loyal followers were killed by the powerful armies of the Umayyad Caliph Yazid. Husain's martyrdom was a very powerful motif in the Iranian revolution, when Iranians exposed themselves to the guns of the shah's army to witness to the Islamic values of social justice, which they believed the shah was violating.

But what we saw on September 11, turning the vulnerability and lonely courage of the martyr into an act of aggression, is a great and wicked perversion, and there is nothing in Islam that can sanction that.

British writer Karen Armstrong, a former Catholic nun, is the author of a celebrated, best-selling account of Christianity, Judaism, and Islam, A History of God, Islam: A Short History, Muhammad: A Biography of the Prophet, *and* The Battle for God, *on fundamentalism in the major religions. She teaches at Leo Baeck College, a seminary for Reform Judaism in London.*

PEACEFUL JIHAD

A DISTINGUISHED LAW PROFESSOR EMPHASIZES THAT ISLAM
BEARS A MESSAGE OF PEACE, NOT VIOLENCE.

By Dr. Khaled Abou El Fadl

When it comes to the issue of Islam and violence, I must confess
that, as a Muslim intellectual, I find myself in a bit of a bind. Islam,
as expounded in the classical books of theology and law, does not
bear a message of violence. In fact, *salam* (peace and tranquility)
is a central tenet of Islamic belief, and *aman* (safety and security)
are considered profound divine blessings to be cherished and vig-
ilantly pursued.

The absence of peace is identified in the Qur'an as a largely
negative condition; it is variously described as a trial and tribula-
tion, as a curse or punishment, or, sometimes, as a necessary evil.
But the absence of peace is never in and of itself a positive or de-
sirable condition. The Qur'an asserts that if it had not been for divine benevolence, many mosques, churches, synagogues, and
homes would have been destroyed because of the ignorance and
pettiness of human beings. Often, God mercifully intervenes to
put out the fires of war and save human beings from their follies.

The Islamic historical experience was primarily concerned
not with war-making, but with civilization-building. Islamic theology instructs that an integral part of the divine covenant given

to human beings is to occupy themselves with building and creating, not ruining and destroying life. The Qur'an teaches that the
act of destroying or spreading ruin on this Earth is one of the
gravest sins possible. *Fasad fi al-'ard*, which means to corrupt the
Earth by destroying the beauty of creation, is considered an ultimate act of blasphemy against God.

Those who corrupt the Earth by destroying lives, property,
and nature are designated as *mufsidun* (corruptors and evil-doers)
who, in effect, wage war against God by dismantling the very
fabric of existence. In addition, the Qur'an states that God has
made people different and diverse and that they will remain so
until the final day. Accordingly, the challenge is for human beings
to coexist and interact despite their differences. The Qur'an pro-
claims in unequivocal fashion, "God has made you into many nations and tribes so that you will come to know one another. Those
most honored in the eyes of God are those who are most pious."

From this, classical Muslim scholars reached the reasonable
conclusion that war is not the means most conducive to getting "to
know one another." Thus, they argued that the exchange of technology and merchandise is, in most cases, a superior course of action to warfare. In the opinion of most classical jurists, war, unless
it is purely defensive, must be treated as a last resort as it is not a
superior moral virtue. Perhaps because of these moral imperatives,
the Islamic civilization excelled in the sciences, arts, philosophy,
law, architecture, and trade—and Islam entered into areas such as
China, Indonesia, Malaysia, the Philippines, and sub-Saharan
Africa primarily through traveling merchants and scholars, and not
through warfare.

Despite this rich doctrinal and historical background, the
dilemmas of a modern Muslim intellectual persist. For one, this tolerant and humanitarian Islamic tradition exists in tension with
other doctrines in the Islamic tradition that are less tolerant or humanitarian. Other classical Muslim scholars, for instance, insisted
on a conception of the world that is bifurcated and dichotomous.

Those scholars argued that the world is divided into the region of Islam (*dar al-Islam*) and the region of war (*dar al-harb*); the two can stop fighting for a while, but one must inevitably prevail over the other. According to these scholars, Muslims must give non-Muslims one of three options: become Muslim, pay a poll tax, or fight.

These classical scholars were willing to tolerate differences as long as the existence of these differences did not challenge Muslim political supremacy and dominance. This dichotomous and even imperialist view of the world, however, did not go unchallenged. For instance, many classical scholars argued that instead of a two-part division of the world, one ought to recognize a third category, which is the region of truce or neutrality (*dar al-sulh*)—a region that is not Muslim but which has a peaceful relationship with the Muslim world.

In addition, many classical jurists argued that, regardless of the political affiliation of a particular territory, the real or true region of Islam is wherever justice exists (*dar al-'adl*) or wherever Muslims may freely and openly practice their religion. It is therefore possible for a territory that is ruled by non-Muslims and where Muslims are a minority to be considered part of the region of true Islam.

A MUSLIM DILEMMA

The fact that the Islamic scholastic tradition is not unitary, and that it is often diverse and multifaceted, is hardly surprising. What is surprising and often aggravating is the extent to which Islamic debates in the modern age have become politicized and polarized. It is difficult for a contemporary Muslim scholar to take a position on Islam and violence without becoming the subject of suspicion and even accusations as to his loyalties and commitments. For instance, if a contemporary Muslim scholar emphasizes the imperatives of tolerance and peaceful coexistence in Islam, or emphasizes the importance of moral commitments over political expedience, or perhaps condemns terrorism, he is often understood to hold a thoroughly political position. Such a scholar becomes susceptible to accusations of being a sellout to the West, pro-Israeli, pro-government, or of being insufficiently sensitized to the suffering of the Palestinians, Kashmiris, Chechnyans, or any other oppressed Muslim population.

The real challenge that confronts Muslim intellectuals is that political interests have come to dominate the public discourse, and to a large extent, moral discourses have become marginalized in modern Islam. In many ways, since the onslaught of colonialism and its aftermath, Muslims have become preoccupied with the attempt to remedy a collective feeling of powerlessness and a frustrating sense of political defeat, often by engaging in highly sensationalistic acts of power symbolism. The normative imperatives and intellectual subtleties of the Islamic moral tradition are not treated with the analytic rigor that this tradition rightly deserves but are rendered subservient to political expedience and symbolic displays of power.

The theology of power in modern Islam is a direct contributor to the emergence of highly radicalized Islamic groups, such as the Islamic Jihad or al-Qaeda. Far from being authentic expressions of inherited Islamic paradigms or a natural outgrowth of the classical tradition, these are thoroughly a byproduct of colonialism and modernity. Such groups ignore the history of the Islamic civilization, with all its richness and diversity, and reduce Islam to a single dynamic—the dynamic of power. They tend to define Islam as an ideology of nationalistic defiance. A vulgar form of obstructionism to the dominance of the Western world. Instead of Islam being a moral vision given to humanity, it is therefore constructed as the antithesis of the West. In the world constructed by these groups, there is no Islam; there is only opposition to the West.

I am not implying that resistance to Western cultural hegemony, or fighting oppression, is illegitimate. But the type of Islam that the radicalized groups offer is akin to a perpetual state of emergency where expedience trumps principle, and illegitimate means are consistently justified by invoking higher ends. What prevails is an aggravated siege mentality that suspends the moral principles of the religion in pursuit of political power. In this siege mentality, there is no room for critical thought or for seriously engaging Islamic intellectual heritage. There is only room for bombastic dogma and for a stark functionalism that ultimately impoverishes Islamic heritage.

JIHAD VERSUS VIOLENCE

This, perhaps, is nowhere as clearly apparent as in the treatment of the issue of jihad and violence. Jihad is a core principle in Islamic theology; it means to strive, to apply oneself, to struggle, and persevere. In many ways, jihad connotes a strong spiritual and material work ethic in Islam. Piety, knowledge, health, beauty, truth, and justice are not possible without jihad—without sustained and diligent hard work. Therefore, cleansing oneself from vanity and pettiness, pursuing knowledge, curing the ill, feeding the poor, and standing up for truth and justice even at great personal risk are all forms of jihad.

The Qur'an uses the term jihad to refer to the act of striving to serve the purposes of God on this Earth, which includes all the acts mentioned above. Importantly, the Qur'an does not use the word jihad to refer to warfare or fighting; such acts are referred to as *qital*. While the Qur'an's call to jihad is unconditional and unrestricted, such is not the case for *qital*. Jihad is a good in and of itself, while *qital* is not. Every reference in the Qur'an to *qital* is therefore restricted and limited by particular conditions, but exhortations to jihad, like the references to justice or truth, are absolute and unconditional. Consequently, the early Muslims were not allowed to engage in *qital* until God gave them specific permission to do so. The Qur'an is careful to note that Muslims were given permission to fight because they had become the victims of aggression. Furthermore, the Qur'an instructs Muslims to fight only those who fight them and not to transgress, for God does not approve of aggression.

In addition, the Qur'an goes on to specify that if the enemy ceases hostilities and seeks peace, Muslims should seek peace as well. Failure to seek peace without just cause is considered arrogant and sinful. In fact, the Qur'an reminds Muslims not to pick fights and not to create enemies, indicating that it is a Divine blessing when one chooses to make peace. God has the power to inspire in the hearts of non-Muslims a desire for peace, and Muslims must treat such a blessing with gratitude and appreciation, not defiance and arrogance.

In light of this Qur'anic discourse, Muslim jurists debated what would constitute a sufficient and just cause for fighting non-Muslims. Are non-Muslims fought because of their act of disbelief or only because they pose a physical threat to Muslims? Most jurists concluded that the justification for fighting non-Muslims is directly proportional to the physical threat they pose to Muslims. In other words, if they do not threaten or seek to harm Muslims, then there is no justification for acts of belligerence or warfare. Similarly, relying on precedents set by the Prophet, classical Muslim jurists held that non-combatants—children, women, people of advanced age, monks, hermits, priests, or anyone else who does not seek to or cannot fight Muslims—are inviolable and may not be targeted.

The existence of these doctrines is crucial for assessing the relationship between Islam and violence. But the reality is that the impact of such doctrines entirely depends on how modern Muslims choose to understand, develop, and assert them. Perhaps it is painfully obvious that regardless of how rich, humanistic, and moral the Islamic tradition is in fact, this tradition will be of very limited usefulness if it is not believed and acted upon by Muslims today.

Herein is the true travesty of modern Islam and the agony of every honest Muslim intellectual. It is fairly well-known that non-Muslims suffer from much ignorance and prejudice about the Islamic doctrine of jihad, its meaning, and its effect. Unfortunately, much of this ignorance is shared by Muslims themselves about their own tradition. For example, many Muslims today do not know the difference between jihad and *qital* or are woefully ignorant about the rules for the conduct of war in Islam. Even worse, when contemporary Muslim scholars rise to emphasize the numerous moral and humanistic aspects of the Islamic tradition, they are accused by their fellow Muslims of being Westernized or of seeking to appease the West.

The real danger is that in this highly polarized and politicized climate, much of what is authentically Islamic and genuinely beautiful will be lost or forgotten for a long period to come.

Dr. Khaled Abou El Fadl is the Omar and Azmeralda Alfi Distinguished Fellow in Islamic Law and a professor at the University of California, Los Angeles School of Law.

SIX MYTHS ABOUT ISLAM

A SUFI TEACHER AND PEACE ADVOCATE SAYS THAT FOR MUSLIMS
AND NON-MUSLIMS ALIKE, IT IS CRUCIAL TO SEPARATE MYTH FROM REALITY.

By Shaykh Ahmed Abdur Rashid

Since September 11, Americans have heard again and again that real Islam means peace; it opposes corruption, terror, and acts based on anger or hate; it stands for security, reconciliation, and love for God's creations. One wonders if such principles truly are well-known to most Muslims. Certainly, the Muslims who support the essential Islam—the Islam grounded in the compassion and mercy of Allah—seem to have been in a minority in vocalizing their faith—although we pray and assume that they are the numerical majority.

Many factors fed the hatred that burst forth that September morning, including decades of poverty, oppression, and conflict; the repercussions of colonialism; the resentments caused by short-sighted foreign policies. But mindful that " . . . Allah does not change [a] people's condition unless they change their own inner selves" (Qur'an 13:11), I would like to focus on a factor closer to home: the misinterpretations that have been allowed to obscure the beauty of Islam.

Islam is drowning in a sea of myths—not just myths held by non-Muslims, but myths contrived by extremists who glorify death and disregard believers' responsibility to work toward a peaceful and contented life for all peoples. We have seen the devastation that results when misguided individuals distort *sharī'a* under the guise of education or promises of retribution. We have seen innocent people suffer because the name Islam has been grafted onto attitudes such as envy, revenge, hatred, selfishness, materialism, tribalism, and disregard for human rights.

MYTH AND REALITY

In the wake of September 11, it may take decades for Muslims to be accepted rather than suspected. We cannot shortcut this process, but we can facilitate it by debunking some of the most widespread myths surrounding Islam.

Myth #1: The worldwide community (*ummah*) of Muslims is monolithic.

Reality: Islam is a universal *dīn* (faith or religion) that has been subject to diverse interpretations.

As a universal faith, Islam offers a living demonstration of qualities to which all human beings can relate: compassion, mercy, tolerance, patience, love. It contains a coherent and deep inner dimension through which individuals may refine themselves and come nearer to a personal and present God-Truth. But bearing the label "Muslim" is no guarantee of living its teachings. Muslims are not a single, homogeneous entity. Grave risks arise from thinking that they are.

Moderate Muslims must make clear the distinction between those who strive toward "inviting to all that is good, enjoining what is right and forbidding what is wrong . . ." (3:104), and those who have spent decades spreading disinformation and offering calculated training in hate. We must counter destructive movements by designing and implementing constructive plans of action. We cannot presume immunity to the viruses of extremism; rather, we need to educate ourselves and future generations in how to diagnose their symptoms and build resistances against them.

Myth #2: Islam is puritanical.

Reality: Islam is an expression of purity and potential.

I need not elaborate on the practices and images that have fostered the myth of puritanical Islam, from women being denied education and being beaten in public to peaceful voices of dissent being silenced through incarceration or execution. But this is not the reality of Islam as I know it. Islam as I know it recognizes a process of inner and outer development accompanied by responsibility, duty, choice, and eventually, humble service.

Humanity is engaged in a process—a process of development and evolution of ethics, morality, character, knowledge, technology, and understanding. This process proceeds best when societies steer clear of dictating unrealistic expectations or goals that are not yet attainable. No person or group can demand of another what even God does not demand. That which has come to be called "fundamentalism" is unrealistic and blatantly wrong in imposing such demands. Its misguided proponents see situations only in black and white. They assume that others can and will change to fit their ideas of religious purity. Much of what they preach is so unfair, compromising, and demeaning that people naturally recoil from embracing it.

The lives and teachings of prophets such as Jesus and Muhammad exemplify the goal of our sojourn in this world. The attainment of this goal cannot be legislated. It certainly cannot be institutionalized. What is revealed and taught speaks to the ultimate capability of certain human beings; but it must also apply in degrees to all people. Imperfections and barriers, failures and renewed effort are all part of the journey.

Myth #3: Muslims are out to convert the world.

Reality: Muslims are guided to be examples of harmony, tolerance, and peace—qualities that attract the human heart.

Although Islam forbids compulsion, certain subgroups of Muslims have demonstrated almost missionary zeal for enlisting converts. Yet *da'wa* (the term used for Islamic outreach) literally means "inviting or calling to," not recruiting. Real *da'wa* aims not to swell the ranks of our congregations, but to encourage celebration of the truth, mercy, compassion, and forgiveness of God, along with respect for all of God's creation. We should come forward with open hands, courage, and a sense of duty to serve those around us. How we act and work creates a passage to the next world. If we act for the sake of Allah, we are complete—let Allah respond as he wills.

The greatest *da'wa* is to respond to the needs of our neighbors, our communities, our society, and our world. We as Muslims have an understanding of universal values like tolerance and justice; we have a progressive and fulfilling way of life. These can be tremendous assets to the people around us.

Myth #4: Islam is fixed, static, and unable to adapt to the contemporary world.

Reality: Islam is a foundation for progress, enlightened development, and dynamic, positive change.

This myth reflects both the postmodern desire to make all rules subject to revision and the orthodox backlash against such revisionism. Islam does indeed call for upholding certain fundamental principles: to help those in need; to be generous, peaceable, and just; to honor the contributions of women as well as men; to respect people of all races and backgrounds. Far from being reducible to rigid dictates, these "absolutes" require progressive thought and action.

The framework of Islamic law—the rules and regulations governing the lives of Muslims (*sharī'a*)—is evolutionary, not constraining. In Arabic, *shaari'* means "a broad street or boulevard." *Sharī'a*, therefore, could be understood as a broad boulevard of activity. It is like a raga in Indian music. A raga is a precise musical form, but endless improvisation is possible within that form.

Sharī'a establishes parameters that support the constructive exercise of choice.

Consider, for example, the issue of organ transplants. Some Muslims may regard organ transplants as an offense against God's natural order, arguing that the violation of a body is forbidden in Islam. But other contemporary Muslims note that according to Islamic law, "the lesser of two evils is to be chosen if both cannot be avoided." From this perspective, an organ transplant is permissible if it will make the difference between life and death.

We need to wrestle with these issues actively, recognizing our current context and the questions raised by ongoing developments. Islam is in need of a revivification, which I believe could come from North America. Muslims here are well-positioned to play a leading role in this great work, for the openness of our society enables us to make the most of Islam's dynamic, values-oriented, spiritually fulfilling yet practical way of life.

If we fail to take responsibility for revivifying Islam—if we remain silent and passive—the arrogant and misguided will continue to speak and act in our name. Already they have worked for years to corrupt the minds of a generation of discontented "have-nots" and to create ideologues out of conflicted educated individuals. To counter their doctrines, we must be equally diligent in using the light of *sharī'a* to relate to today's world in ways that can benefit the human community.

This effort is the real jihad, in contrast to the kind of jihad associated with the next myth.

Myth #5: Jihad refers to military confrontations, and Muslims launch such wars for any number of reasons.

Reality: The concept of jihad reflects a realistic understanding of the inner and outer need for struggle, with the goal in all instances being peace.

We all know that the word jihad does not refer primarily to "holy war." Jihad literally means to strive or struggle. Muslims, at least, should understand the meaning of jihad. We should understand deeply the full potential of striving to perfect the expression of truth in our lives, for in this inner striving lies a key to averting outer struggles and conflicts.

When we set selfishness aside, we become better able to accept graciously what God has given us, be it gold or iron, poverty or wealth. We find refuge in patience. We stop blaming others and become humble enough to look at ourselves, to see our faults, repent, and try to rectify the wrongs we have done to those around us. We begin to consider others' needs as if they were our own. Then, we can help to create peace in our outer world.

To be a Muslim is by definition to be a person who actively works for the peace, security, and the well-being of all people. Yes, Islam permits the use of military force—in some cases, Islam commands defensive combat—but always, the use of force must support long-term peace.

What are Muslims permitted to defend? The freedom to say, "Our Lord is God," to remember God often, to worship in security, whether in a mosque, church, synagogue, or temple (22:39–40). How are Muslims to respond to attacks? Proportionately. "If you have to retaliate, let your retaliation be commensurate with the wrong done to you" (16:126). Forbidden is the destruction of an enemy's family or livelihood. When should Muslims make peace? As soon as the enemy offers peace, even if the overture may be a ruse (8:61–62). Finally, while the oppressed have the right to take "an eye for an eye," forgiveness is considered more praiseworthy and more beneficial in the long run (42:36–44).

The Prophet Muhammad himself set an example of repelling evil with that which is better. Through years of persecution in Mecca, he and his companions never resorted to armed resistance. At Hudaybiyah, the Prophet again demonstrated the power of nonviolent tactics. When Mecca's polytheist rulers refused to let the Muslims make their pilgrimage, some of the Prophet's companions called for battle. Overriding their wishes, the Prophet Muhammad signed a treaty. Shortly afterward Allah revealed, "Lo! We have given you a clear victory . . ." (48:1). The Treaty of Hudaybiyah is what people today might call a "win-win" outcome. It set the stage for the Muslims to later take Mecca without shedding a drop of blood.

One of the most successful modern-day practitioners of nonviolence was the Muslim leader Khan Abdul Ghaffar Khan, who, in the 1930s and 1940s, mobilized the Pathans of the North-West Frontier (now Pakistan) into a nonviolent army on behalf of Indian independence. His success reflected the *hadith*: "Allah grants to gentleness what He does not grant to violence."

Sustainable security, prosperity, equity, and peace depend on addressing more than geopolitical issues. Accords that emerge from the United Nations or The Hague may lead to a cessation of violence. But ongoing coexistence depends on the reconstruction of society, which can only take place in an atmosphere where trust, love, faith, understanding, and economic and religious security can develop.

We have seen how dangerous longstanding resentments, cultural biases, and prejudice can be—how they may be usurped by opportunists and power-hungry egotists who grasp a bit of the truth, then culture it in the petri dish of discontent into a toxic weapon of mass destruction. So deadly is the weapon they devise that it destroys both its intended target and those that create or employ it.

Without question, millions of Muslims are suffering today. The majority of the world's refugees are Muslims. UNICEF estimates that sanctions against Iraq have contributed to the deaths of five hundred thousand children. In the Philippines, the Balkans, Nigeria, and elsewhere, Muslims are struggling. These are terrible situations, and we stand with our brothers and sisters in these lands.

But as we consider how Muslims can best respond to oppression and conflict, we should look at the meaning and application of jihad with the same creativity that we bring to topics like medical ethics, technology, or entrepreneurship. Islam has never been a religion of the sword. Our challenge is to reflect Allah's attributes in our lives.

We are not alone in striving to translate spiritual values and qualities into daily life. We have allies among the sincere believers of other faiths. In order to tap the power of these alliances, we need to combat a final myth.

Myth #6: Relations among Jews, Christians, and Muslims are inherently hostile.

Reality: Tensions among Jews, Christians, and Muslims can be resolved.

Islam supports religious tolerance. According to the Qur'an, "Those who believe—the Jews, the Christians, and the Sabaeans— whoever believes in God and the Last Day and does what is right—surely their reward is with their Lord . . ." (2:62). Historically, many Muslim governments treated religious minorities well, honoring their religious, legal, and economic structures; encouraging their scholarly contributions; and welcoming them into the military, the civil service, and positions of government office.

That said, relations among Muslims, Jews, and Christians are undeniably tense in parts of the world today. The ongoing Israeli-Palestinian conflict has significantly soured Muslims' attitudes towards Judaism and toward supporters of the state of Israel. In addition, many Muslims, especially outside the Western world, have been kept ignorant of the unifying teachings of Islam and consequently harbor cultural and religious prejudices against Christians and Jews.

But we Americans are not ignorant of these teachings. Like the Prophet—who had Jewish neighbors and business associates; whose wife's cousin was a Christian; who was respected by Christian monks and who in turn praised and respected the Christian ruler of a neighboring country—we, too, know Christians and Jews who share our values. It is time to affirm our common interest in combating the extremism that plagues all three Abrahamic faiths. It is time to replace arrogance with dialogue, saying, "God is our Lord and your Lord. To us our works and to you your works; no argument between us and you . . ." (42:15).

DEFINING OURSELVES

While myths abound, so, too, do opportunities for talented, open-minded, and visionary Muslims to bring forward Islam's positive potentials. We need to support those among us who are best able to express the true Islamic worldview, based in tolerance, equity, compassion, generosity, patience, justice, and peace. As we try to find our way out of present circumstances, we must not shirk our personal responsibility, our moral foundation, or our duty to look critically at the tracks in the sand before they disappear—to see from whence we came and to look ahead to the horizon, toward where we are headed.

Let us go forward with our hands extended in sisterhood and brotherhood to all as peacemakers, reconcilers, seekers after knowledge, and givers of hope. Other people may define us with their words. Let us define ourselves through our actions and contributions.

Source: The commentary on organ transplantation is based on the article "Organ Donation and Transplantation," posted online by the University of Northumbria (UK) Islamic Student Society at www.unn.ac.uk.

Shaykh Ahmed Abdur Rashid, an authorized teacher in five Sufi orders, is founder of the Circle Group, which works actively to apply the principles of Islamic Sufism to current issues through programs in education, peace building, leadership training, and cross-cultural relations. He lectures frequently at universities, interfaith forums, and conferences on topics ranging from nonviolence to faith and democracy.

HOW MUSLIMS CAN COMBAT TERROR AND VIOLENCE

A MEMBER OF "MUSLIMS AGAINST TERRORISM" SAYS A NEW GENERATION OF AMERICAN MUSLIMS AREN'T JUST SPEAKING OUT AGAINST TERRORISM—THEY'RE DOING SOMETHING ABOUT IT.

By Aasma Khan

I do not want to touch the scar that is so lightly healed. I can still feel the pain and horror of the September 11 attacks if my mind dwells on that day of tragedy. Inside my head, I can still see the planes crashing into the World Trade Center Towers. This injustice, this loss of innocent lives, has seared my soul and in each retelling, the grief still does not easily subside. My eyes can still well with tears.

People who claimed to be Muslims committed those crimes against humanity. How is that possible? Islam is a religion of peace. I do not want terrorists to cloak themselves in Islam. I do not want them to take the names of Islamic Jihad (Holy War) or Hezbollah (Party of God) or al-Qaeda (the Principle), all names with religious significance. I do not want them to claim Islam at all. They do not represent Islam. They represent the worst of what humanity is capable of—and they say they do it for God.

What these terrorists do in the name of religion is *not* Islam. The Qur'an says, "Whosoever kills an innocent human being, it shall be as if he has killed all mankind, and whosoever saves the life of one, it shall be as if he had saved the life of all mankind" (5:32). Moreover, the Qur'an prohibits suicide. It says, "Nor kill or destroy yourselves, for God has been most merciful to you" (4:29). It does not take a scholar to figure out from these simple textual references that Islam prohibits the taking of innocent lives in suicide attacks.

EDUCATE TO ERADICATE IGNORANCE

I, along with twelve other young Muslim-Americans, decided in the aftermath of the attacks that we would no longer let Osama bin Laden and others of his ilk lay claim to Islam and pervert it. We declared on our Web site, "Our mission is to stand up, as Muslims, against those who preach hatred and violence in the name of Islam and to promote peace and understanding through interfaith and intercultural coalition building. We are tired of extremists dictating the public face of Islam. We are committed to mobilizing the silent majority of Muslims, a majority which is in favor of peace, tolerance, and mutual respect."

We formed Muslims Against Terrorism on the Sunday after the attacks. We have made our declaration and taken Islam back, and though our numbers have started small, our message has spread to people from more than ninety countries. We have grown from just thirteen young professionals to more than seventy.

Unlike existing Muslim organizations, we engage in education about Islam for both Muslims and non-Muslims. We do not proselytize. We are focused on educating about the incompatibility of Islam with terrorist activities, hatred, and violence. Accordingly, we have begun programs of: 1) adult education about Islam; 2) children's education about Islam; 3) Muslim education to eliminate confusion about Islam's message of peace; 4) press education to eliminate misinformation in coverage of Islam; and 5) our Web site, www.matusa.org, to reach anyone interested in learning about Islam and its message of peace.

Our educational focus drives us to reach out to the best of humanity, the best of who we are, the best of Islam. We strive for a dialogue with everyone, with every faith that carries within it compassion, understanding, and respect for differing beliefs. Thus, in the example of our Prophet Muhammad, we make a promise to all who engage with us in dialogue that we " . . . approach one another with love and understanding, patience and respect, humility and self-criticism, rationality and reasonability, with open hearts and open minds in the pursuit of peace." This is our mission.

By raising the discourse from laying blame and finding fault to one of understanding and compassion, we have created a space for Muslims to challenge the ills plaguing our society as Muslims and all societies in the world. Confronting terrorism—for the Muslim community—is just the beginning. We must also confront bigotry, racism, and gender apartheid. All of these social ills have found refuge in what we call cultural Islam. Cultural Islam takes cultural practices that exist outside of Islam and attempts to make it a part of Islam.

By facing the ills confronting the Muslim community, true Islam—its ideals, its hopes, its promise—will emerge. By confronting intolerance and hatred, we delegitimize the message sent by terrorist attacks. Instead, we must stand for justice, even if it is against ourselves (Qur'an 4:135). When we achieve justice for all—women, men, black, white, yellow, brown, red, Muslim, non-Muslim—we make it possible to forge a lasting peace. Our method is to give everyone the knowledge to understand Islam and start a dialogue. By providing this education, we hope to delegitimize the messages of hatred and intolerance sent by terrorist attacks.

To accomplish these goals, we have presented not only at public schools, private schools, and youth camps but we have also begun the important project of teaching teachers. This will make a lasting change in the way Islam is taught and understood. We have traveled to churches, synagogues, temples, interfaith centers, and college campuses. We have assisted corporations in diversity training to include Islam and understand what Muslims practice. We have reached out to our own community to provide the educational materials needed to explain Islam's prohibition on the taking of innocent lives in suicide attacks. We have talked to imams and Muslim student associations and made contact with other major Muslim organizations to share our message and materials. Last, but certainly not least, we try to educate the press and prevent the publication of misinformation about Islam. In all formats, Muslims Against Terrorism uses educational tools and dialogue as a means for addressing the challenges that face our society. All our programs teach the true, tolerant nature of Islam, its prohibitions against violence, and its respect for diversity in all its forms.

A TASK FOR EVERY MUSLIM

Every Muslim can do this. They do not need to belong to this organization to talk about the peaceful message of Islam to anyone. Every Muslim needs to take responsibility for their Islam and claim it, own it, and defend it from those who would defile God and all his religions by killing innocent lives in his name. I do not mean to say that all Muslims are responsible for the September 11 attacks or any other terrorist attacks. I do mean to say that every Muslim has a responsibility to explain Islam so that everyone can be better educated about it. We must step out of our shells instead of staying hidden away. We must stop hoping someone else will do something about those terrorists.

The terrorists feed on our fear. Fear is founded on ignorance. Muslims fear non-Muslims and vice versa. Our bridge is education. Building bridges is hard work. Often there is not even a foundation on which to build, just a hope that it can be done. Every day, everyone at Muslims Against Terrorism looks forward with hope, working to accomplish justice and find peace. But it is a long journey. It is daunting. Inside, I worry that I do not know enough—about myself, about my religion, about other religions—to step forward and take on the threat that terrorists pose to humanity with their intolerance and hatred. Even though I do not feel ready, I take the step forward anyway. I see my fellow Muslims Against Terrorism members standing beside me and take heart. "I" becomes "we." The "we" grows larger with each step. We must stand against this oppression. We will not be silenced. We will face our fears. Will you join us?

Aasma Khan is a practicing attorney and the spokesperson for Muslims Against Terrorism (www.matusa.org).

DEMOCRACY

A merican commentators sometimes claim that Islam and democracy cannot coexist. To back up this statement, they point to the numerous dictatorships thriving today in Muslim lands. But how many pause to recall that a lot of those lands (including modern-day Iraq, Lebanon, and Syria) were created—and saddled with puppet sovereigns—by European democracies after World War I? For an authoritative look at this issue, see Karen Armstrong's compelling essay, "Can Religious States Be Democratic?"

As Alexander Kronemer writes in "Islamic Democracies," "The greatest obstacle to democracy in the Muslim world is not 'Islam.' It is poverty, the lack of education, and corrupt and repressive regimes, many of which—and this is the important point—are supported by the democracies of the West." Kronemer also quotes a protest chant that has the ring of 1776, though in fact it was coined in Morocco ten years ago: "They didn't consult us (the people)! They didn't consult us! / The decision belonged to us (the people)! / They didn't consult us!"

It is absurd to think that people anywhere would not like more of a say in their government, if they could have it. Absurd, too, is the notion that a religion prevents them from having it. In America, Muslims have settled in comfortably, thank you, to lobbying Congress and getting out the vote. There is simply no evidence that being a Muslim and being American are inherently contradictory.

How easily many Americans forget that their own democracy did not emerge full-grown without a struggle. In fact, American democracy developed slowly over many decades, a product of
give and take and occasional painful conflicts that more than once
spilled over into bloodshed and tragedy—the Civil War, the
murder of Dr. Martin Luther King Jr., for example. Even now, it
seems unwise to view democracy and freedom as accomplished
facts. Their price remains vigilance.

Today, American Muslims are learning that price, too, as guilt
by association runs through the land, casting long shadows on
some of them and on their institutions. Omid Safi, in "Being
Muslim, Being American after 9/11," underscores the importance
of a Muslim critique of the current official program summed up
as "The War on Terrorism." "For us," he writes, "it is a 'space in the
middle' because it means critiquing both U.S. foreign policy and
the actions of some groups marked by Muslim identity, such as al-
Qaeda."

This "space in the middle" is also the topic of Salam al-
Marayati's essay, "The Rising Voice of Moderate Muslims." He
notes that this concept is expressed in the Qur'an: "We have willed
you to be a community of moderation" (2:143). Perhaps the blink-
ered mullahs of al-Qaeda skipped reading that chapter altogether.

CAN RELIGIOUS STATES BE DEMOCRATIC?

A RENOWNED HISTORIAN CITES TRADITIONS AND EXAMPLES OF DEMOCRACY IN THE ARAB WORLD.

By Karen Armstrong

Democracy is not created by an act of will. The form we know today emerged very gradually in the West. It was not simply dreamed up by political scientists or inspired statesmen but appeared as the result of a process of trial and error. Over time, we've found it to be the best way to run a modern society.

In the sixteenth century, Europe and what would later become the United States began to create an entirely new kind of society. In what we call the premodern world, all civilizations were based economically on a surplus of agriculture, which could be used for trade. But at the time of the scientific revolution, the West began to create a society founded on technology and reinvestment of capital, enabling Europe and America to replicate its resources indefinitely.

This involved major change at every level of society, and it was a painful process. Modernity did not come fully into its own until the nineteenth century, and during that time the Western countries experienced revolutions, violent wars of religion, exploitation of workers in factories, the despoliation of the countryside, and great distress as people struggled to make sense of this profound change. Similar upheavals are going on now in developing countries, including the Islamic countries, as they make this difficult rite of passage.

The new order demanded change on every level: social, political, intellectual, scientific, and religious. And the emerging modern spirit had two main characteristics: independence and innovation.

There were declarations of independence in nearly all fields. The American Declaration of Independence was a modernizing document, and the war with Britain a modernizing war. But people also demanded independence intellectually: Scientists could not permit themselves to be impeded by a coercive state or religious establishment; the Protestant Reformers who declared their independence of the Catholic Church were also forces for modernization. And innovation figured in this: Constantly people were making something new, breaking unprecedented ground, discovering something fresh. There was excitement as well as the distress that inevitably accompanies major change.

It was found that in order to be fully productive and thus provide a sound basis for the new civilization, more and more people had to acquire the modern spirit and therefore a modicum of education, even at a quite humble level. Printers, clerks, factory workers, and finally women were brought into the productive process. As the populace became more educated, they quite naturally demanded a share in the decision-making process of society.

Similarly, to make full use of its human resources, governments found they had to draw upon minority groups such as the Jews, which had been either persecuted or confined to ghettos in Europe. In England, Catholics were emancipated. Those societies that were secular and democratic seemed to work best. In Eastern Europe, countries that reserved the fruits of modernity for an elite, and that used more draconian measures to bring Jews into the mainstream, fell behind. It's important to note that this modernization took about three hundred years. New ideas and ideals had time to filter down to society's lower echelons, under the dynamic of its own momentum. This has not been the case in the Islamic world. Here, modernization has been far more accelerated, leaving no time for the trickle-down effect. Consequently, society has been polarized: Only a privileged elite has been educated to take part in modern politics while the vast majority find their society changing in ways that seem incomprehensible and bewildering. It has been compared to the trauma of watching a beloved friend changed by mortal illness. Religion has been a solace—but of course religion, too, has to change in the modern world.

In some Islamic countries, furthermore, modernity has not been accompanied by independence, but by colonial subjugation. Even after colonialism, powers like Britain or France, and latterly the United States, continued to control the political destiny of these developing nations. Instead of independence, we've seen an unhealthy dependence. Secondly, instead of innovation, the Islamic world has had to settle for imitation. We are simply too far ahead.

Islam is not inherently opposed to democracy, however. The attack of September 11 was not a war against democracy or freedom. There are principles in Islamic law, such as the need for *shura* (consultation) before passing new legislation, which would be very compatible. And it is not strictly true that Islam is incapable of separating what we in the West call church from state. In practice, Muslims have perforce kept religion and politics separate. In the Shi'ite world, this separation of religion and politics was a sacred ideal because all states were seen as corrupt. In the Sunni world, there was a de facto separation of religion and the political life of the caliphal court. The *shari'a*, rules and regulations governing the lives of Muslims, began as a counterculture, as a white revolution against what they saw as the corruption of the court. The *'ulama'* (religious scholars) promoted a more egalitarian, principled, and just system of law than was actually feasible in the realpolitik of the court, which had its own aristocratic culture, known as the *Adab* (courtesy, good manners). Some Muslims do have semantic problems with the Western definition of democracy: "Government with the people, for the people, and by the people" is not tenable because from an Islamic perspective, God— and not the people—is sovereign.

And there are historical difficulties to contend with. Early last century in Iran, the leading intellectuals and progressive *'ulama'* demanded a modern constitution and representational government. A parliament *majlis* was duly set up by the Qajar shahs but never allowed to function properly. First the Russians helped the shah to close it down; later the British, who were trying to make Iran a protectorate during the 1920s, rigged elections to ensure a result favorable to themselves. In 1953, the CIA and British intelligence were instrumental in restoring to the throne the deposed Shah Reza Pahlavi, who not only closed down the *majlis* to effect his modernization program, but systematically denied Iranians fundamental human rights.

In Egypt, there were seventeen general elections between 1923 and 1952, all of which were won by the popular Wafd party, but the Wafd were permitted to rule only five times. They were usually forced to stand down by either the British or the king of Egypt. So democracy has got a bad name, and sometimes even seems like a bad joke.

Nevertheless, as modernization progresses, some Muslim states may realize—as Western countries did before them—that a degree of democratization and secularization are essential. This seems to have been Iran's experience. The Islamic Revolution of 1978–1979 did give Iranians forms of representational government for the first time; admittedly, these institutions were flawed and often highly unsatisfactory, but a start had been made.

At the very end of his life, Ayatollah Khomeini made an important "declaration of independence," proclaiming that the state must have a "monopoly" in such practical matters as urban affairs, agriculture, or the economy and must be emancipated from the

constraining laws of traditional religion and the conservative mullahs. Government, he said, must not be impeded in its utilitarian
pursuit of the interests of the people and what he saw as the
greater good of Islam. He also seemed to support the radical
sermon preached on January 12, 1988, by the speaker of parliament, Hojjat ol-Islam Rafsanjani, which announced that Iran must
strive for a form of Shi'ite democracy, rooted in God.

So the achievement of a full democracy is not simply a
matter of setting up a parliament, and it is nearly always contested.
Religion can sometimes facilitate the struggle. After the American
Revolution, the prophets of the religious revival known as the
Second Great Awakening used the New Testament to demand an
equality and a greater share of power for the people than some
aristocratic Founding Fathers had envisaged. Religion can be a
modernizing factor, and some forms of fundamentalism in the
Middle East can be seen as enabling people to make the painful
rite of passage to modernity more easily.

*British writer Karen Armstrong, a former Catholic nun, is the author of a celebrated,
best-selling account of Christianity, Judaism, and Islam,* A History of God, Islam: A
Short History, Muhammad: A Biography of the Prophet, *and* The Battle for God,
*on fundamentalism in the major religions. She teaches at Leo Baeck College, a seminary
for Reform Judaism in London.*

ISLAMIC DEMOCRACIES

ACCORDING TO A FORMER STATE DEPARTMENT OFFICER,
THE QUESTION IS, DOES THE UNITED STATES REALLY WANT THEM TO EXIST?

By Alexander Kronemer

Can Islam embrace democracy? This basic question and others like it have become the titles of countless news shows, articles, debates, and panel discussions. Can Islam be pluralistic? Does Islam tolerate free speech, free association? Does it allow voting and elections? When President Bush addressed the nation after September 11, saying that "they" hate us because of our freedom and our democracy, is the reason "they" hate freedom and democracy because of Islam? Or to ask the big question lurking behind all of this, Is Islam the new global threat to the West, the new Soviet Union?

Few questions are more important in shaping our calculations about the future of the world. Yet, if understanding the future is the goal, the question is wrong.

Islam is a religion. It is a sacred history, a holy scripture open to varying interpretations and practices. Islam cannot embrace, welcome, or tolerate. Only Muslims can. And the fact is that hundreds of millions of Muslims already do embrace democracy, while many millions of others daily risk everything to obtain it. The notion that Islam and democracy are somehow incompatible is belied by Bangladesh and the 129 million Bangladeshis who participate in one of the world's largest parliamentary democracies. And by Indonesia, the world's largest Muslim country, which is making progress from a long-entrenched authoritarian regime to a more pluralistic, representative democracy. And by India, where nearly 200 million Muslims live and participate in the world's largest democracy.

It is also belied by the many Muslims listed every year in reports from Amnesty International and Human Rights Watch who are jailed, tortured, and in some cases killed as they work to bring about democratic reforms to the largely secular, authoritarian regimes that still dominate much of Africa, the Middle East, and Central Asia.

There are, of course, Muslims whose interpretation of religious tradition leads them to reject democracy. The theological argument being that in democracies, the will of the people is supreme, whereas under a true Islamic regime, the will of God, as revealed in the Qur'an and by the example of the Prophet Muhammad, should be paramount.

There are also avowedly Islamic regimes that are staunchly authoritarian. Yet, even for those Muslims who maintain that the Qur'an must have primacy in government, Muslims have found ways to give it a democratic interpretation. The world's other famous radical Islamic regime, the Islamic Republic of Iran, has democratic institutions and functioning elections.

It may sound odd to refer to Iran as a democracy. After all, the government—more "moderate" though it may be—still aims to frustrate many United States foreign policy goals in the region. The greatest obstacle to democracy in the Muslim world is not "Islam." It is poverty, the lack of education, and corrupt and repressive regimes, many of which—and this is the important point—are supported by the democracies of the West.

Nearly fifty years of Cold War history have accustomed the West to viewing the world as split into two basic camps: either democratic and totalitarian. In that world, democracies were almost by definition friendly and pro-American, while authoritarian Communist regimes were generally anti-American. Similarly, within the world's democracies, those working to overthrow them usually had strong anti-American sentiments, while within various authoritarian regimes, the pro-democracy elements were also pro-American.

Then in 1978 came the shot heard around the world that prefigured a new paradigm: The Iranian Revolution. That a populist uprising against a despotic regime could also be virulently anti-American was an utter shock—though it shouldn't have been a surprise given the longtime support the United States gave to the hated shah. Suddenly, the West was confronted by the voice of the people of a region who viewed the United States as economically, politically, and culturally predatory.

The Iranian Revolution showed us that democratic movements, particularly Islamic ones, could be anti-American. Thus, about a decade later, when the democratically elected Islamic Party in Algeria was summarily overturned by a military junta, igniting one of the world's cruelest civil wars, hardly a word of protest was uttered in Washington, D.C., and other Western capitals.

During the Gulf War, this new voice was briefly expressed in popular demonstrations in Rabat, Tunis, and Algiers that were ultimately quelled. Once more, disagreement with United States policy and a yearning for democracy were joined as, for example, Moroccans marching to protest the bombing of Baghdad on February 3, 1991, chanted:

> *Ma sa'alunash! Ma sa'alunash!*
> *Al-qarar qararna!*
> *Ma sa'alunash! Ma sa'alunash!*

> *They didn't consult us (the people)! They didn't consult us!*
> *The decision belonged to us (the people)!*
> *They didn't consult us! They didn't consult us!*

Does anyone today doubt that, if allowed, the democratic will of the people of Jordan or Egypt or Saudi Arabia would lead to a decidedly less favorable reception of United States foreign policy aims than is currently afforded by the friendly autocrats in the region?

There is a temptation, when asking the big questions about the Muslim world, to revert to Cold War thinking and see ourselves in conflict with an ideology—once Communism, and now Islam. But what we are really facing is people. People who, when given a voice, express many more different interests, attachments, and affinities than our own. What is Baghdad to the average American but the place where the hated Saddam Hussein wields his power? But to the average Arab, it is a centuries-old center of art, literature, and culture. It is a name that conjures memories of a glorious history and which holds a cherished place in the imagination. Of course Muslim Arabs (and Christian Arabs) are going to oppose its bombing and demand a different solution to the problem than one that causes grave destruction to such a beloved place.

The question is not whether "Islamic ideology" will allow Muslims to embrace democracy and freedom. The writing is already on the wall: Muslims are intimately familiar with the ideals of freedom and democracy and by and large embrace them. Democracy will continue its spread around the world. The irony is that despite almost universal rejection of United States foreign policy by the "Muslim street," that same constituency has great admiration and praise for American democracy and freedom.

So it is not how we confront an ideology, but how we respond to people's newly expressed concerns that will shape the nature of the years to come. Are we going to help bring about democracy in the Muslim world, or be remembered (and resented) for our opposition to it through the support of a hated regime? At what point do we stop promoting our interests with regional autocrats and take up the principle of promoting freedom and democracy? How do we weigh morality and expediency?

In the end, these are primarily questions about United States ideology, not Islam. From the moment the Declaration of Independence defined the soul of America by establishing the principle of democracy for all, U.S. history has been defined by the struggle to embrace this ideal. The Civil War, the Women's Suffrage Movement, prejudice against various immigrant groups, the internment of Japanese Americans, and the Civil Rights movement—all are examples of this struggle. Did freedom for all include the poor, slaves, women? After resistance and conflict, America has always finally answered "yes." As new constituencies emerged and their voices could no longer be ignored or easily co-opted, they had to be taken into account, included in the vision of freedom.

Now the question is: Does this principle include the Muslim world, particularly the Muslim-Arab world? In a region where expedience is the surest way to secure our interests, are we ready to take into account the voices of people whose interests may differ from our own? In the end, the question for the future is not whether Islam can embrace democracy. It is whether we can.

Alexander Kronemer, a former State Department officer in the Office of Democracy, Human Rights, and Labor, is currently coproducing a documentary on the life of the Prophet Muhammad for public television.

BEING MUSLIM, BEING AMERICAN
AFTER 9/11

A SOCIAL CRITIC ON WHY PROGRESSIVE MUSLIMS
MUST NOT BE SILENT ON UNITED STATES HUMAN RIGHTS ABUSES.

By Omid Safi

*"And thus have We positioned you as a community in the
middle, so that you may be witnesses onto humanity."*
—Qur'an 2:143

Terror, terror, terror. Terrorist, terrorist, terrorist. War on terror. War
on terrorism. This barrage of phrases comes at us with mind-
numbing frequency. Russia, Israel, and China have now hijacked
the language of "war on terrorism" to combat their own oppressed
citizens and neighbors.

Beyond its undeniable emotional appeal in light of September 11, the war on terrorism remains ill defined. What are its
aims, apart from the vague promise to "root out terrorists"? Who
determines what groups constitute terrorists, beyond those responsible directly for the crimes against humanity of September
11? How will it move from a unilateral United States show of
force to a truly global quest for justice? When, if ever, will this war
on terrorism end?

In the post-September 11 era, the space for public dissent and discussion of this "war on terrorism" continues to shrink. The minute one stands up to question its logic, its target, its victims, its methods, one is accused of treason: "You are being unpatriotic." Yet it is critical for American Muslims to insist on precisely such a space. For us, it is a "space in the middle" because it means critiquing both U.S. foreign policy and the actions of some groups marked by Muslim identity, such as al-Qaeda.

We speak for the dignity of human life, all human life, no matter what race, religion, or nationality. We speak for the inalienable right of all of God's children to live in peace and security. We criticize both the hideous actions committed by Muslim extremists and the hypocrisy of our own American government in putting profit before freedom, foreign policy interests before human rights.

This "space in the middle" is not a popular or easy place to be. Many Muslims will not be pleased to hear my criticism of some Muslim communities. Some may even go so far as to accuse progressive Muslims of having "sold out." Some non-Muslim Americans will object to my criticism of United States foreign and domestic policy. Many will see this as being unpatriotic in a time that the nation still needs healing and unity.

Since September 11, I have been told repeatedly, "We must stand by our president." I politely, firmly, passionately, and compassionately disagree. I love my children very much, much more than I love our president, and yet I criticize some of their actions. I criticize them not because I wish to abandon them, but precisely because I love them.

I see a difference between nationalism and patriotism. If nationalism implies that I somehow identify more with the citizens inside a national border than with those outside of it, I will not abide by this "ism." My identification is with all of God's children, the American and the Russian, the South African and the Indian, the Israeli and the Iranian, the Palestinian and the Chinese. As complicated as identities are, I aim to identify with the "children of Adam"

(Bani Adam), as the Qur'an calls the universal community of humanity. Patriotism, on the other hand, is different. To me, patriotism is about upholding the ideals upon which this great nation was founded, even if those ideals have not always been perfectly adhered to. I write this essay as an American Muslim, committed to pursuing social justice and peace for all of God's creatures. I write this as a patriotic American Muslim who calls on both Muslims and Americans to strive for the highest ideals of our traditions, while adopting self-critical perspectives. I call on us to rise up and be counted.

A PLEA TO MUSLIMS

Let me start with my Muslim brothers and sisters. It has been difficult to be a Muslim in America since September 11, with the constant bombardment of images about "terrorists" and "suicide bombers" associated with us. Yet, I call on my Muslim friends—whom I love so dearly—to rise above this and take responsibility for ourselves and for our communities.

The typical pattern for many Muslims, both in the United States and abroad, has been to lay the blame for our social and political malaise at the feet of this or that foreign entity, be it "the British," "the Americans," "the Jews," "the Hindus," or "the Communists." It is time to stop the blame game, to take responsibility. We are in charge of our destiny, we are in charge of our families, and we are in charge of our communities.

Far too long, we have sat silently—I have sat silently—when someone gets up in our Islamic centers, our mosques, and vents poison. How many foaming-at-the-mouth, hate-filled speeches about "the Jews" and the "corruption of women" and the immorality of "the West" have I heard in our sacred spaces? Enough is enough. No more shall we divert attention from abusive situations, class warfare, and institutional injustice by directing our wrath at various other enemies. It is time for Muslims to be true to our destiny, bringing justice, peace, and compassion to that one race to which we all belong: humanity.

I am tired of being always spoken for, but never speaking. I am tired of hearing people like Osama bin Laden telling us that being Muslim means killing Americans, and I am tired of President Bush telling us that Islam is peace. While the second is more pleasing to my ears, I know—and I suspect all honest Americans know—that Muslims have their saintly souls and their zealots, just as every other tradition. I will not settle for the simplicity of either perspective but push ahead for something more complex and real, something that approaches the subtlety and complexity of the lives of more than one billion Muslims.

I am tired of turning on CNN and MSNBC (and, worse, Fox "News") and seeing every quack and charlatan all of a sudden becoming an "expert." I am tired of seeing policy makers who pontificate on affairs that have life-and-death consequences for the citizens of these regions, yet they have never stopped to look into the eyes of the human beings whose lives they are impacting. I am tired of hearing the disciples of Samuel Huntington and his vile "Clash of Civilization" theory fill posts in the State Department and attempt to turn Islam into the new anathema after the fall of Communism. I am tired of seeing book after book of the historian Bernard Lewis, repeating his rant that dismisses all Arab encounters with modernity as failed and weak. I am tired of all this nonsense.

I want to hear 1,001 Muslim voices, agreeing, arguing, covering every point on the spectrum. I want us to figure out what Islam is, what it can be. To speak is to have power; to be silent is deadly. I do not expect all of us to agree on everything, but I do expect us to talk intelligently and compassionately, and to listen, and to be heard.

A PLEA TO AMERICANS

Let me now address my fellow American citizens. I have less and less faith in a political system that seems to have been hijacked by an assortment of special interest groups. I do have faith, however, in the basic decency of most Americans. I call on Americans to demand that our government lives up to the great ideals upon which it was founded. Our nation has strived for freedom and human rights. We have at times fallen short of these ideals, with the horror of slavery, the treatment of Native Americans, among other sins. At other times, we have nobly dared to dream the loftiest, particularly with our humanitarian work after World War II and during the Civil Rights Movement. Yet most Americans are unaware of the way our government's foreign policy has so frequently departed from the pursuit of the very ideals that our nation is built upon. Far too often, we have put the pursuit of the dollar before the pursuit of dignity. While this hypocrisy—let's call it what it is—has been the case in so many regions of the world, it has particularly characterized our interaction with the Muslim world.

Yes, it is true that no other nation has committed so much to humanitarian causes. Yes, it is true that American soldiers time and again stand up as peacekeeping forces in many regions. It is also true, sadly, that our own government time and again has supported corrupt tyrannical dictators in many parts of the world. One can point to many examples in the Muslim world. For example, in 1953, the CIA sponsored a coup in Iran to remove the democratically elected prime minister, Mohammed Mossadegh. What was his crime? He wanted to claim Iranian oil for Iranians. So our own government trampled over the principles of democracy in order to once again make a buck in oil. In place of Mossadegh, the United States reestablished the monarchical rule of the Shah of Iran, who ruled as a dictator. Is this what a democratic nation like the United States should be supporting?

And this is not an isolated case. In the beginning stages of the "War on Terrorism," our government secured the support of Parvez Musharraf, the military dictator who took over Pakistan in a coup. In order to secure his compliance, we promised Pakistan billions of dollars in military aid. Is this what a democracy like the United

States should be doing? Is this wisdom, arming both the Pakistanis and the Indians with billions of dollars of military equipment when twice in the past few years they have gone to the verge of nuclear war? Why is it unpatriotic of me to ask my government to apply the standards of democracy, freedom, and human rights in its dealing with foreign countries?

The hypocrisy of U.S. foreign policy goes on and on. Since the 1930s, the government that I pay my taxes to has supported the Saudi Arabian monarchy, the same regime that uses its petro-dollars to export its brand of Wahhabi Islam around the world. This is the same Wahhabism that is a literalist, extremist interpretation that has attempted to exile all soul and spirit from Islam. The same Wahhabism that is responsible for the oppression of so many of my Muslim sisters. Why on Earth would our own government be supporting the Wahhabis and their regime? One word: oil. Saudi Arabia is the third-largest producer of oil consumed in the United States, and so long as there is a drop of cheap oil under the sands of Saudi Arabia, our government will turn a blind eye to the human rights violations in Saudi Arabia and in other countries that import Wahhabi ideology. As long as the financial interests of the United States oil companies count for more than justice and human dignity, we will hypocritically support the Saudis.

Let's be more specific. We engaged in a massive bombardment of Afghanistan, an already poor country utterly devastated by our assault. We used the most powerful types of nonnuclear bombs. In doing so, we killed thousands of innocent Afghani civilians who had nothing to do with September 11, nor did they have anything to do with harboring terrorist groups like al-Qaeda. In attacking the Taliban, we have pointed out how they have imposed the worst type of gender segregation on its citizens and made life a living hell for Afghani women and children when they were in power. But here is my point: If we object to the Taliban's inhumane version of Islam, why do we not object to the root source of the Taliban's interpretation of Islam? Taliban ideology is nothing but Saudi Wahhabism, mixed in with Pakistani Secret Police and a dash of CIA military training. Why do we blast the bastard child of Wahhabism to the Stone Age while continuing to turn a blind eye to the source of fanaticism, the Wahhabis in Saudi Arabia? Again, one word: oil.

RECLAIMING ISLAM

We American Muslims want our faith back, as a spiritually powerful means of transforming ourselves and our world. We want our democracy and our civil rights back. In the months after September 11, perhaps one thousand Arabs and Muslims were detained without being formally charged with crimes. And then there is the racial profiling of Arab-American communities in Michigan and elsewhere, so benignly called voluntary interviews by the FBI. Is this how we treat other religious and ethnic minorities? After Michael Bray attacked abortion clinics, did we round up all evangelical Christians who follow the Army of God movement? When Timothy McVeigh blew up the federal building in Oklahoma City, did we round up all members of the Christian Identity movement? Or is it somehow more acceptable to do this to American citizens who are Muslim because they are not "really American"?

I will not sit silently and accept the absurd detention of Afghani prisoners in Guantánamo Bay in Cuba. Surely there are some real terrorists among them, some al-Qaeda soldiers who must be brought to justice. The international community has a legal process for this: the International War Tribunals at The Hague. Why do a mass of Arab and Afghani suspects continue to be held without representation in Cuba? Among the hundreds held there are many Afghani tribesmen who were caught up in political games more complicated than they realized but who in no way, shape, or form supported the atrocious terrorist actions of September 11. Why are they not classified as "prisoners of war"?

And if they are prisoners of war, they must be entitled to Geneva Convention rights. Yes, I realize the irony of insisting on civil rights even for those who set out to destroy the symbols of American life. But I will not accept trampling over internationally agreed-upon rights in order to save those very rights. The ends do not justify the means.

Time and again I have heard people argue that "these are desperate times, and they call for desperate measures." The absurd and painful truth about the above is that I have never seen a person say, "These are desperate times, so please take away my civil rights. Please come and search my home. Please hold me for month after month without charging me with a crime. Please single me out in airport security." Of course not. They mean that it is okay to take away Arab or Muslim civil rights.

STAYING PUT IN THE U.S.

From time to time, I hear from people who say, "If you disagree with U.S. foreign policy, get the hell out." I am not leaving. I was born here, and my children were born here. I love the promise of America, the goal of what it can be, too much to leave it. I hold this as the responsibility of a patriotic citizen. I am a social critic not because I hate America but because I am committed to seeing us live up to our lofty ideals. I will abandon neither my faith nor my commitment to the patriotic ideals of America.

My parents migrated to America not because they were ashamed of their own homeland of Iran and not even because they were looking for financial reward. Our family has deep roots in Iran that go back centuries, and we were quite well-off there. We moved to this country because of the promise of freedom and human rights. My family still believes that this is the one country where human beings are born with the possibility of pursuing human dignity without oppressive and draconian measures imposed by the government.

I will work with my fellow progressive Muslim brothers and sisters to reform Islam in this complicated world. Let us as progressive Americans also insist on an America that we can be proud of. We will insist on this "space in the middle," from which we can find inspiration in the highest ideals of Islam and America while painfully and honestly offering our critique when we act contrary to those ideals. The Qur'an calls the community of Muslims "a spiritual community of the middle, to be witnesses for humanity" (2:143). Today, during the "war on terrorism," being a Muslim of the "middle community" means being a witness, calling both Muslims and Americans to the highest good of which we are capable.

Caught in the middle we are, alone and frightened, but silent we will not be. Let us speak with conviction and compassion, concern and courage, and pray that other like-hearted progressive souls will join this middle community.

Omid Safi is a professor of Islamic Studies at Colgate University. His research focuses on Islamic mysticism (Sufism).

THE RISING VOICE
OF MODERATE MUSLIMS

A PROMINENT ACTIVIST SAYS MODERATION IN ISLAM IS LIKELY
TO IMPROVE THE OUTLOOK OF MUSLIMS WORLDWIDE.

By Salam al-Marayati

When we speak of the rising voice of moderate Muslims, there are two important points: that it is rising because in the past it has been the silent majority, and that it is an authentic moderate voice as a result of acting in accordance with the Qur'an, not against it.

These two points are critical to the policy-making process and, therefore, to America's image and interests in the Muslim world. There exists a healthy and eager segment in Muslim countries interested in dialogue and constructive engagement and in serving as a bridge between our society and the Muslim world. This voice is central to a more effective and representative United States policy toward that region.

Some observations on the moderate voice are in order. The moderate voice is not an elitist or Westernized voice. It is not a lonely or persecuted voice. And it is not a purely secular voice. It is a voice of the Muslim mainstream, grounded in a Qur'anic verse: We have willed you to be a community of moderation (2:143) and in the admonition of the Prophet Muhammad to stay away from extremism.

There are Muslim extremists, just as there are Christian and Jewish extremists. That is different from saying, however, that there is a split in Islam. Unfortunately, moderates are at times defined as those who are not religiously observant or who are fighting, even repressing, other Muslims. Nevertheless, the focus must remain on the interests at stake: ending the scourge of global terrorism, promoting Middle East peace, and preventing nuclear conflicts. Consistency on human rights and democracy will help us achieve these goals. The moderate Muslim voice does not acquiesce to issues of freedom and justice. It is the inevitable voice of the future.

The word "reform" is found in the Qur'an. In Arabic, it is called *islah* and is the root meaning of the word *maslahah*, which means the public interest. Historically, Muslim intellectual leaders such as Farangi Mahall Wali Allah, Jamal al-Din al-Afghani, and Muhammad Abduh are among the most notable Muslims who have used reason to create revivalist movements. Wali Allah of India helped to reopen the gates of *ijtihad*, individual reasoning, and condemned the blind imitation of tradition. Al-Afghani challenged Muslims to think of Islam as consistent with reason and science. Abduh believed in educational reforms throughout Muslim society.

These same concerns are raised today with respect to the plight of Muslims as illiteracy, poverty, and a lack of effective political systems create an environment that is more susceptible to criminal activity. One challenge for Muslims today is to shift from the paradigm of the colonial model, which perpetuates the notion of Jews and Christians as agents of colonialism. The perception that globalization is merely a tool of Western imperialism results in antagonism instead of efforts of change within Muslim society.

One concern about Islamic political movements is the apprehension that they will come into power with an antidemocratic orientation. As a reflection of support for the status quo, the official United States government response to date has been to remain silent when these groups are suppressed within authoritarian Arab regimes. When that suppression takes place, however, it leads to more radicalized groups. Prevention of dissent in Saudi Arabia led to bin Laden's rise in Afghanistan and the formation of al-Qaeda. Despite the fact that these radical groups are real and are ongoing, the moderate voice, while remaining alive, has not been heard.

When five hundred thousand Muslims rallied in Pakistan in October 2001 for peace and moderation, it was a footnote in the press reports. In that rally, statements against terrorism and for tolerance were made, yet attention remained fixated on the few who burned effigies. After September 11, Muslims from around the world expressed shock and remorse over the terrorist attacks, ranging from a moment of silence during a soccer match in Iran to candlelight vigils throughout the occupied territories of Palestine. Statements of solidarity with the American people coupled with condemnations of the terrorist attacks were sent from practically every Muslim country.

Lack of widespread hostility toward Americans and even many aspects of American culture is one feature of mainstream Muslims. On a more substantive level, however, is the yearning for self-government and freedom, a sentiment found on the streets of every Muslim city. To some, a form of Islamic democracy is a means to achieve those goals. The moderate Muslim voice is based on the need for equity, a civil society within each Muslim country, and rapprochement with the West on the global level.

Some may say that the expressions of moderation and support for the United States are made for political expediency, for survival. But, to many Muslims standing firm against terrorism, it is an Islamic obligation. In principle, Islam has no room for terrorism. In practical terms, more Muslims die from terrorist attacks than any other group, whether instigated by Muslim extremists or Christian, Jewish, Hindu or Buddhist extremists.

The prognosis for Muslims worldwide is bleak. Conditions are more ripe for anarchy and lawlessness than stability and economic advancement. Refugees emanate from Muslim countries more than any other part of the world. The Muslim masses want Islam to be a vehicle for change. While terrorism has become a problem in the Muslim world, it is erroneous to explain this problem of violence as one rooted in Islam or Islamic thinking. Rather, the Muslim world turns to religion as respite from economic hardship, political instability, and other consequences of failed states.

It has become popular to quote verses out of context from the Qur'an to argue that warmongering and terrorism are central to Muslim belief and practice. Those who perpetrate violence in the name of Islam distort and abuse the texts in the name of their causes, but the texts themselves are not to blame and should not be the subject of scrutiny since legitimate Muslim scholarship utterly rejects the aberrant interpretations. The Qur'an and *hadith* are clear in terms of supporting conflict only as a last resort in order to defend oneself against clear military aggression. Numerous restrictions apply, including the prohibition against killing civilians, destroying buildings, and fighting other Muslims.

Because many Muslims seek forms of government that incorporate Islamic law to one degree or another, the concept of *sharī'a* needs more thoughtful approaches in United States policy making. *Sharī'a* is a core of laws that comprise basic principles (based on the Qur'an and *hadith*) and man-made laws. Imposing *sharī'a* violates the Qur'anic injunction: Let there be no compulsion in matters of faith. The notion of religious police, therefore, violates this code. The exploitation of *sharī'a* leads to persecution of religious minorities and women.

There is this oversimplification done by both self-proclaimed experts and Muslim extremists that use *sharī'a* as a political football fixating on the penal code and not the call for government responsibilities—for example, to be accountable to the people through a social contract. The five goals of *sharī'a* accepted by all Islamic jurists are to secure and develop life, mind, faith, property, and family. These are consistent with human rights declarations and the United States Constitution. In a national conference held by the Muslim Public Affairs Council, one speaker presented the thesis that the U.S. Constitution is the closest human document that fulfills the goals of *sharī'a*. His message was well-received by all one thousand participants.

While it is wrong to impose the *sharī'a* on non-Muslims or Muslims against their will, it is also wrong to disallow Muslims, who seek *sharī'a* as a way of advancing their societies, from participating in political affairs. Legal systems based on *sharī'a* already exist in many parts of the Muslim world. To suggest that the only acceptable form of government involves the absolute separation of church and state is to ask for more tension and rejection.

Other challenges are facing Americans interested in United States policy in the Muslim world. All citizens of this great country cherish the values of freedom, human rights, and justice. But those values are not perceived to be America's foreign policy goals.

For effective counterterrorism policy to take shape, terrorism must be viewed as a global problem. It is wrong for rogue states and extremist groups to use it, and it should be wrong even if our allies use it. Double standards, however, will impede our progress in counterterrorism policy. Hindu militants, such as the Tamil Tigers, caused the greatest amount of terrorist fatalities in the 2000 report on patterns of global terrorism. Kahane Chai, the Jewish extremist group that was founded in America, has links with the Jewish Defense League, which has allegedly aimed to eliminate moderate Muslim voices, including leaders of the Muslim Public Affairs Council. They were actually successful in killing Alex Odeh of the American Arab Anti-Discrimination Committee in 1985. His assassin remains at large to this day. And when the Irish Republican Army was on the terrorist list, it was given room to allow fund-raising for its political wing, Sinn Fein. When the United States government is viewed as soft on terrorism with some groups, the result is an undermining of U.S. credibility among the masses.

While the moderate Muslim voice opposes the double stan-

dard, it rejects the extremist exploitation of the legitimate grievances among the Muslim masses. It is time to talk specifics, especially in terms of advancing the human conditions of people,
including people of all faiths, in the Muslim world. We must come
with reasonable and constructive stands on how to resolve the
Palestinian-Israeli conflict. Coexistence is essential for Jewish and
Muslim people to gain security for themselves, and let's not forget
that Christians in the Holy Land have been reduced to a fraction
of their original population since the Israeli occupation of the West
Bank and Gaza began in 1967. It is not realistic to expect peace
while not expecting the end of Israeli settlements or of the military occupation. Nothing shapes the psyche of the Muslim world
more than the events related to the Palestinian issue, and nothing
else impacts America's image in the Muslim world as much as the
Palestinian problem.

In dealing with Muslim countries, Muslim groups, and the
Muslim masses, it is important to recognize that the use of reason,
a pillar in the foundation of our secular society, is not alien or
modern to Muslim cultures. The Qur'an stipulates that the use of
reason is one of the commandments of God, alongside justice and
decency. The Qur'an also challenges people to use reflection, and
it defines itself as a book made for those who think.

It is time to include American Muslims in not only the cele-
brations in Washington but also in the difficult discussions that will
affect the future of the United States and the world. I feel privileged to be a Muslim living in America, as many American Muslims do. We can live Islam according to our human understanding
and be responsible American citizens at the same time. This expression can be admired and gain the respect it deserves from
Muslims worldwide.

*Salam al-Marayati is the executive director of the Muslim Public Affairs Council
(MPAC), based in Los Angeles and Washington, D.C.*

NO MORE SIMPLISTIC ANSWERS

AN AMERICAN SHEIKH SAYS LIFE ISN'T BASED ONLY ON LAW;
MUSLIMS SHOULD EMBRACE THE "GRAY AREAS."

An Interview with Taha Jabir Alalwani by Radwan A. Masmoudi, Ph.D.

*Taha Jabir Alalwani grew up in Iraq. After graduating from
Al-Azhar University in Cairo in 1959, he returned to Iraq,
where he became a professor and imam. He later returned to
Cairo, earning a doctorate in 1972. He then taught Islamic
jurisprudence in Saudi Arabia for eleven years. In 1984, he
helped establish the International Institute of Islamic Thought
(IIIT) in the United States. He now teaches at the Graduate
School of Islamic and Social Sciences in Leesburg, Virginia,
where he is also the chairman of the Fiqh (Jurisprudence)
Council of North America.*

**What are the main challenges facing Muslims in the twenty-first
century?**

Muslims need to know themselves and know others. They don't
know who they are, what their role in life is, and what kind of relations they should have with others. They tend to choose naïve
and simplistic answers. They like to summarize everything by
saying it is *haram* (forbidden) or halal (allowed). But *fiqh* (jurisprudence) is not everything. It is only one aspect of life. Life is
not based on law alone. You have legal, economic, social, and political needs. The majority of Muslims, in the West and abroad,

think it is enough to say this is *halal* or this is *haram*, this is okay, this is not.

Some of us think life is only a path to death, and that all you need to do is take short cuts to *al-Janna* (paradise). What about life itself? Allah tells us we are his vice-regents on Earth, and he gave us his trust. He gave us certain responsibilities. In the Qur'an, Allah says, "He who created you from this earth and gave you the responsibility to build it."

Our task is to build a civilization with values. Unfortunately, this concept is absent from our lives. Muslims now have an "individual" mentality. They think of the need of the individual not the *ummah*, or community, needs. In our religion, we have many obligations to the community. You must have hospitals, doctors, engineers, schools, roads, food, etc. These obligations fall on the community. The individual must cooperate with others to fulfill these requirements. Muslims think, by mistake, that if you pay to build a mosque, you will get more reward from Allah than if you pay to build a hospital, for example. A Muslim can feel the link between the mosque and Allah, but he or she can't feel or see the link between a hospital and Allah, in the same way. This also applies to other societal needs such as housing students, publishing books, or building an institution fighting against dictatorship and calling for *shura* and democracy.

This is a misguided and distorted understanding of Islam. We need to rebuild our concept of life and help Muslims understand their role in life and how to have a balance between life and the hereafter. How to build a strong *ummah* or community? This is the big challenge and the responsibility of the elite of this *ummah*. Anyone who has some education must do his or her best to help the *ummah* understand these needs.

What about the concept of an Islamic state? Is there such a thing as an Islamic state, and how would you define it?

I would like to be very frank on this issue. In all of my studies, I never felt that Islam was too concerned about building a state.

Islam, from the beginning, was working to build an *ummah*, and there is a big difference between building an *ummah* and building a state. Building an *ummah* means you have certain concepts and values. The Muslim *ummah* is based on three main values: *tawhid* (oneness of God), *tazkiya* (purification of the human being), and *'imran* (building a civilization with values). These three values are considered as the main goals of Islam. When you build an *ummah* on *tawhid*, *tazkiya*, and *'imran*, you will have a strong *ummah*. *Ummah* means a community built around certain values.

For example, the founders of this country left Europe and came here with certain values. They did not find room to implement those values in Europe, so they decided to find another place. They came here with their values to build this country. This is an *ummah*, and not a nation, because a nation is built around a piece of land, not values. This means that God does not want to be governor or mayor. God created us and gave us certain values. He told us if you like to fulfill your duty on this Earth, you must follow these principles. The details of how to build your political or your economic system are up to you. God has not appointed a caliph (leader) for us. It is up to us, the *ummah*, to appoint a caliph, but this caliph cannot be responsible for everything. He must be guided by the *ummah*, through a parliament or *majlis al-shura*, and he must be accountable to the *ummah*.

This understanding of the sovereignty of God is part of the legacy of the children of Israel, not the Islamic legacy. In the beginning, Allah decided to lead this experience by himself. He told his people, "I am going to build you as a model. Your land is a sacred land, you are my nation and my people, and I will be your governor and leader. Your prophets and messengers will be my assistants." That's why when you read the Old Testament, you find that their relationship with Allah was a relationship between a people and their leader, not their God. For example, they asked him *We need lentils, we need onions, we need this, and we need that.* When they asked for water, Allah said, "O, Moses, hit the stone with your cane, and you will get water." He did, and every tribe got their own water.

The relationship with God was based on miracles of the unseen. Then, the people became dissatisfied, distrustful, and bored with that. When they saw other people worshipping a cow, they said *We need a God we can see*, so the as-Samiri (the tempter) made a cow for them. Allah mentioned those stories in the Qur'an as lessons.

Unfortunately, some colleagues from the Islamists misunderstood the stories. They thought that sovereignty of God still applies, and Muhammad, like Moses, came to implement sovereignty of Allah. No, he did not. He did not even talk about it.

What about the verse that says, "Whoever does not rule according to Allah's wishes are the unbelievers"? Many Islamists use this to justify the need for an Islamic state.

That verse means rule according to Allah's teachings as *ummah*. This means you have to develop the system to implement those values. Your obligation is to implement justice. How? It is your business. I need from you to build freedom. How? It is your business. I need from you to establish fairness and trust. How to do that? It is the business of the community, the *ummah*.

The message of Islam is not for a specific nation. It is impossible to develop a political system for the whole world and put all of humanity under one system, regardless of differences in languages, cultures, backgrounds, ethnicities, etc. The message of Islam is a message for all humanity. If we try to put all human beings under one system or kingdom or dictatorship or whatever, no one will accept Islam. But, Allah says *I have these values I want you to implement*. You should develop a system, according to your own needs, to implement these values.

When we attempt to develop a system according to our needs, there will invariably be different interpretations. How do we resolve these differences?

Islam teaches us that we need to agree on certain values, but the system is up to us. The system is something under our *ijtihad* and our understanding. When you neglect the *ummah*, the whole nation, and take your decision by yourself, what does that mean? That means you think you don't need the *ummah* and the people. You are highest and you are above them. The Qur'an says, "Man becomes an oppressor because he thinks he is highest." That means when the governor or ruler starts to think that his people are inferior to him and that he does not need them, they should stop him and get him away from power. Why? Because he will cross all the lines and become a dictator. You don't need to wait for him until he says like Pharaoh did, "I don't know any other God for you except me."

From the beginning, we should put the ruler under certain laws and restrictions to help him see the picture in a proper way. If he says, "I am responsible before Allah," we should tell him, "No, you are responsible before the people." If we use these three values—*tawhid*, *tazkiya*, and *'imran*—to build our system, we will never allow a dictator to come to power riding a tank or forcing the people to accept him as a leader.

I remember on August 2, 1990, when Saddam Hussein invaded Kuwait. I was in Egypt. Many people around me were very happy to see Saddam invade Kuwait. I told them, "He will never succeed because the Qur'an teaches us that 'the oppressors will not reach my covenant' and that 'Allah does not guide those who are oppressors.' When you practice this kind of dictatorship and oppression, you will never be able to succeed in the long run."

One of problems that some Muslims have with democracy is the rule of the majority. They say we don't have to follow the majority because the majority can be wrong. Therefore, the rule of the majority is not required. What do you think about this?

This is wrong. Sometimes, Muslims look at one part and forget the other parts. I call this the jurisprudence (fiqh) mentality because as a *faqih*, I always look at the small details of the case and forget about the others. But when you look at the whole picture, you will find something else. Allah told us to implement justice, truth, trust, purification, civilization, etc. This responsibility falls on the *ummah*, which means the majority and not the minority.

If there is any protection from Allah, it is for the majority not the minority. Prophet Muhammad said, "My Ummah will never agree on wrongdoing." There are about eighteen *hadiths* like this, about the guidance and protection from Allah to the *ummah*. The *ummah* always reaches the truth, but the minority sometimes reaches the truth and sometimes misses it. The Prophet said, "You should follow the majority [*Sawad al-atham*] of the *ummah*." That's why the concept of *ijma'* (consensus, unanimity) should be revived to move away from individual and minority rule.

But if we don't have a unanimity (*ijma'*)? Is it okay to accept the majority?

It is better to accept the majority than to accept a minority. If I follow the majority, I am always on the safe side. Following the minority will open the door to other minorities to take over by claiming to know the truth. We can't open this door because it will lead to unspeakable violence and confrontations.

A major hurdle facing the Muslim world today is dictatorship or lack of freedom because it does not allow people to discuss different ideas, strategies, and approaches and to evaluate solutions. Are you optimistic about the ability of Muslims to overcome this hurdle? And how do we get out of this situation?

When we look at history, we find that dictatorship in Europe's history was much stronger and harsher than dictatorship in our countries. With time, however, Europeans developed an acute awareness about this problem. Unfortunately, in our heritage we have some "viruses," and the dictators always use them. When I was a student in Egypt, Jamal Abdel-Nasser invited some of the writers and journalists to speak with him. He told them, "Some of you were talking before the revolution about justice coming through a just dictator; I see some of you now objecting to my role. Why? I am a dictator but I am also just!" This concept was, unfortunately, even mentioned by [Jamal al-Din] al-Afghani himself when he said that the Muslim *ummah* needs a "just dictator." Allah told us there is no way to put these two together. There is no justice with dictatorship. You cannot have both. This kind of thinking needs to be changed in the minds of Muslims.

Finally, do you have any advice for [Muslims interested in democracy in America]?

I feel you have a very difficult task ahead. America and the West can help in many ways, but it is difficult because our culture and our mentality are based on Islam. If you don't bring new ideas through Islam itself, those ideas will be resented and rejected. In Saudi Arabia, for example, America from time to time raises its voice about the need to implement democratic reforms. Saudi officials reply that our religion talks about *shura*, and we have a *majlis* for *shura*, and we don't need anything else because this is our culture and mentality. Even religious leaders and scholars can't accept democracy because they see it as foreign to Islam. We therefore need to try to find something from our legacy and from our heritage and ask them to implement it. Yes, certain groups may raise some objections, but they are much more likely to accept the proposed reforms if we can show them that they are from our own religion and heritage and not in contradiction with it.

Radwan A. Masmoudi, Ph.D., is founder and executive director of the Center of the Study of Islam and Democracy (CSID), a Washington, D.C.-based nonprofit think tank. He is also the editor-in-chief of the Center's quarterly publication, Muslim Democrat.

WOMEN AND ISLAM

The subject of Muslim women—their rights, role, etiquette, and dress—remains one of the great sources of misunderstanding for mainstream Americans. It is of great concern to Muslim women, too, especially *hijab*, the head-covering sometimes accompanied by a long robe that many Muslim women choose to wear. It also marks an area of difference, or preference, among American Muslim women, some of whom choose to dress in a more Western fashion, reserving the scarf or *hijab* for times of prayer only.

Mainstream Americans in general are confused by *hijab*, construing it as a form of male oppression, despite living in a culture themselves that continually seeks new ways to exploit each inch of women's bodies. Muslim women are not uncritical fans of mainstream culture. Some are sharply opposed to it, judging that its freedoms are not worth the high price of its detractions—from marketplace exploitation to date rape and a high divorce rate. If, like most people, you find yourself lost at times in the thicket of such contradictions, this section of essays by and about Muslim women will help you through.

It is surprising how little American feminists have tried to understand the actual circumstance of their American Muslim sisters, and vice versa, when each group is plainly concerned with many of the same issues. Women and men of whatever faith would do well to read Kecia Ali's essay, "Rethinking Women's Issues in Muslim Communities." Rather than quote religious texts, Ali reviews with open eyes the different positions Muslim women hold in Islamic society, their rights, etiquette, and dress. Using the same neutral approach, she clearly illustrates Western culture's misunderstandings of the same subjects.

There are real women's voices here, voices like Ilham Hameedduddin's, who makes light of how some people view her in a scarf and robe: "Neighbors are surprised I can speak English without an accent. They assume I'm fresh off the boat and I just haven't assimilated yet." Or Cynthia Sulaiman, who operates a Muslim Homeschooling Resources Network: "We have mothers who are strictly stay-at-home and very conservative, women who are doctors and scientists, and women who publish magazines for other women. It all depends on what individual women feel they can contribute." Or Samer Hathout: "Some of the most serious problems that American Muslim women face include domestic violence, abuse of divorce and child custody laws, abuse of the polygamy system, and isolation and exclusion from various aspects of Muslim life." Except for the word "Muslim," this sentence could describe any group of women almost anywhere on Earth.

Male chauvinism is another central topic here, as Muslim men and women struggle to rid their mosques of centuries of male domination. Saraji Umm Zaid's essay, "Why Every Mosque Should Be Woman-Friendly," describes a view shared by many of this essential challenge. Then, if you thought every topic to do with Muslim women must be sociopolitical, examine the pages of Halima Touré's essay to be reminded that Islam, like all religions, is mostly concerned with discovering, and recovering, your soul.

RETHINKING WOMEN'S ISSUES IN MUSLIM COMMUNITIES

A FEMINIST RESEARCHER TALKS ABOUT MARRIAGE, MODEST DRESS, AND THE EQUALITY OF THE SEXES

By Kecia Ali

The issues facing the majority of Muslim women around the world today are those facing the majority of women everywhere: poverty, illiteracy, political repression, and patriarchy. At the same time, there are now and always have been elite Muslim women, with wealth and clout, who have exercised power and autonomy within social and economic institutions. No one can argue that these women all share a special status. For this reason, stereotypes of Muslim women as uniquely oppressed bear little resemblance to reality. Yet the attempt to define "women's status in Islam" persists.

Some people take the question about women's status to be about an idealized Islam—mostly referring to Qur'anic and prophetic tradition, sometimes including jurisprudence. As with Christian scripture, analyzing isolated passages from these sources is not likely to give an accurate portrayal of women's rights, nor do these sources necessarily reflect actual practice. A focus on the Qur'anic verses that specifically address women is, however, one common means of attempting to answer the question, "What is women's status in Islam?" Indeed, Muslims have often encouraged this approach as a way of deflecting criticism about women's actual disadvantages in some Muslim societies. Faced with clear evidence of oppression, Muslim apologists state that such practices are contrary to "true Islam," which they claim liberated women from their disadvantaged position in pre-Islamic Arabia. An opposite reaction is heard from detractors of Islam. When women achieve social prominence and personal success in Muslim societies, these critics contend that it is despite Islam.

In order to make any headway in understanding Muslim women's lives—and what is needed to make them better—one needs to move beyond simple arguments. Islam is not the solution to all Muslim women's problems, nor is it the cause of them. I suggest, in fact, that Islam is not directly related to many facets of most Muslim women's lives. Let's take the most striking example, the terrible situation of women in Afghanistan under the Taliban. Where the Taliban's interpretation of Islam was the explicit justification for oppressive restrictions on women's mobility and education, "Islam" does not by itself come close to explaining women's experience under the Taliban. In order to comprehend women's situation in Afghanistan, one needs to understand not scriptural passages concerning women, but rather decades of devastating war, tribal rivalries, lack of agriculture, high infant mortality rate, and so on. While Islam must be analyzed as part of the larger picture, it is meaningless outside Afghanistan's specific historical and geopolitical context. The burka (head-to-toe covering) is less relevant to Afghan women's misery than sheer, crushing poverty.

That is not to say, however, that the burka is a nonissue. Without falling into the trap of assuming, as some Western commentators seem to, that women's dress is a barometer through which status can be measured (the less skin showing, the lower the status), I would suggest that it is related to a constellation of issues that are common to Muslim women—a focus on women's dress, restriction on the mixing of the sexes, and the granting to husbands of significant legal and customary authority over their wives. Although there have never been universally agreed-upon rules on these subjects, nor have regulations been uniformly applied to all Muslim women across time and class boundaries, they are among the crucial issues that shape communities and families throughout the Muslim world—including Muslims in the United States.

ISLAMIC DRESS

Some scholars have shown how debates over Islamic dress have turned it into a potent symbol for "authentic" Islam, at the same time making it a marker of idealized gender difference. Others have suggested that it represents a practical compromise strategy for women who wear it as a means of being taken seriously, not harassed, and allowed more personal freedom without being viewed as unchaste. In this model, women's adoption of *hijab* is a demonstration of autonomy. Still others have suggested that any use of "the veil" is ultimately self-defeating because it carries such powerful connotations of women's subordination and the idea that women's only proper place is in the home. A few have noted that the concept of *hijab* originally referred to a physical barrier of separation from unrelated men for a woman in her home. This idea of a portable "screen" that allows wide mobility and interaction with men outside the family is a very different concept. Of course, seclusion in the premodern era was an elite affair only. The rest of the population relied on the free movement of women from the lower classes. In this sense, contemporary Islamic dress is an egalitarian phenomenon, available for the price of a scarf.

In any event, in the United States and other Western nations, women's head-covering takes on a very different meaning. It is one thing to wear a scarf and *abaya* (robe) in Saudi Arabia, where such dress is compulsory, quite another to do it in Egypt or Kuwait, where women's dress spans the full range from fully covered—including face veil and gloves—to chic and potentially revealing skirts and jeans. It is still another thing entirely to adopt a head-covering in a nation where Muslims are a small minority of the population and the *hijab* itself makes the wearer noticeable.

Three views on the scarf seem to have taken root among Muslims in the West. One calls for wearing the scarf as absolutely necessary, based on Qur'anic and prophetic tradition. In this view, other considerations are irrelevant, and other views are summarily dismissed. A second view argues that women's modesty is critical and that the point of the covering is to make a woman's appearance less the focus of attention. Thus, in the United States, wearing a scarf accomplishes precisely the opposite of the Qur'an's original intention. A third view shares elements with the others. Its proponents recognize both the need to be modest and the specific issues associated with veiling in the United States. They suggest that there are social reasons to veil here—it makes women less a sex symbol and more of a human being and it makes her recognizable as a Muslim—even though some do not consider it obligatory.

Some considerations, generally left out of discussions of veiling, are important to my view that wearing *hijab* needs to be a personal decision made in good faith according to a woman's own understanding of God's commands. At one mosque I attended, I was told that some women's purses had been gone through, during prayers, in order for others to check whether they were properly covered in their driver's license photographs. Muslims may be the first ones who need to stop putting so much emphasis on women's dress and sex segregation, and far more on other aspects of men's and women's moral development—like respecting the privacy of others. Just as we ask non-Muslims not to judge by appearances and assume that a women's headscarf implies oppression, Muslims need to realize that a woman who does not cover her head is not necessarily any less observant or faithful than one who does.

The Qur'an verse most cited in regard to women's dress (24:31) is preceded by an exhortation to men to "cast down their gazes" (24:30). If Muslim women are not allowed to wear swim-suits at the beach, but it is perfectly acceptable for Muslim men to look at and interact with non-Muslim women in bikinis, does this not violate the spirit as well as the letter of the Qur'anic injunction? Muslims need to think of modesty and modest behavior as both male and female duties. Finally, the Qur'anic and prophetic evidence regulating women's dress is far less precise than many assume.

Nonetheless, rather than spending more time and attention focused on how exactly to interpret these texts, I would hope that it would be a nonissue, at least until the other pressing problems facing Muslim communities are resolved. One of the most pressing issues is that of family law.

FAMILY LAW

One common view of *shari'a* rules on marriage and divorce deems them particularly harsh and unfair to women. This view is held not only by non-Muslims but also by many Muslims, particularly in the numerous countries that impose some version of "Islamic Family Law" or "Personal Status Codes," purportedly based on classical Islamic law.

A contrary view is gaining prominence, however. Its proponents argue that, in fact, women are guaranteed numerous rights by Islamic law, but they simply need to learn how to protect themselves by invoking them. The most important way to do so, in this view, is to place conditions in a marriage contract. A wife can thus ensure that she is permitted to work, to visit her family, or to obtain a divorce if her husband takes a second wife. But these conditions are a matter of significant dispute in classical law. And several conditions routinely praised as a means for women to obtain rights are deemed by the majority of classical Islamic jurists void and unenforceable, thus making women's "right" to include them in their contracts meaningless.

For Muslim women in the United States, the situation is different. American Muslims are not subject to a particular interpretation of Islamic law by government decree but rather may choose, as a matter of conscience, to follow certain doctrines. In these circumstances, the legal strategy of including conditions in a marriage contract can be an extremely useful way of making clear the spouses' expectations for the marriage and their roles within it. A prenuptial contract enforceable by United States courts can be an effective method of protecting certain rights, particularly payment of dowry, a wife's right to work (or not to work), and the rights of the spouses to maintain separate property.

In my view, these types of measures are useful as a means of gaining acknowledgment of rights that are recognized by classical jurisprudence but ignored by contemporary Muslims in positions of authority, such as the local imams who draw up marriage contracts. Ultimately, however, these types of conditions do little to alter the traditional imbalance of spousal rights in classical law. For example, there is no condition a wife can include to restrict her husband's right to repudiate her at any time, for any or no reason. This is his unalienable right according to the unanimous view of classical jurists. Of course, in the United States, the spouses would still have to go through civil divorce proceedings before the government would recognize the divorce. Rather than simply picking and choosing from among the doctrines of established legal schools, what is needed is a more thoroughgoing legal analysis with an eye to developing a new, more egalitarian Islamic law.

There is resistance to this type of work on numerous fronts. I will address only what I believe to be the major obstacle: the assumption of many that *sharī'a*, or rules and regulations governing the lives of Muslims, is the same as "Islamic law." The use of the term *sharī'a* in descriptions of legal doctrines as well as national legal codes promotes this confusion. Contrast this with the term *fiqh*, literally meaning "understanding," that is the Arabic word for jurisprudence. The legal schools have historically demonstrated significant variability in method and doctrines; they differ substantially on numerous points of law. These differences are not, as some have suggested, merely matters of detail.

I will give a few examples of how real the consequences of this confusion can be for women. The Shafi'i school allows a wife to obtain a divorce on grounds of nonsupport after as little as three days; the Hanafi school never does, even if the wife is indigent and her husband fails to support her for decades. The Maliki school allows a father to contract a marriage for his never-married daughter over her objections even if she is a thirty-five-year-old professional; conversely, the Hanbali school says that the father's power to force a girl into marriage ends when she turns nine. Virtually all Sunni jurists consider a triple repudiation given at once to be legally effective, if reprehensible; Shi'ite law, however, counts such a pronouncement as only a single divorce. These mutually contradictory positions cannot all be equally correct interpretations of an infallible Divine Will. All, however, are significantly shaped by the patriarchal constraints of their times of origin. Once Muslims recognize this, the need for qualified Muslims to create a renewed jurisprudence should be clear.

COMMUNITY CONSIDERATIONS

The biggest question now is how will American Muslims face these issues? There is an understandable desire not to add to the stereotypes non-Muslims have of Muslim women's oppression. As a result, in discussions with outsiders, Muslim women tend to minimize some very real experiences of being marginalized. While women's experiences within Muslim communities do not come close to being as oppressive as is popularly imagined, neither are they as rosy as some claim. While clearing up misconceptions is important, it should not come at the expense of women having a chance to really confront those issues that are of concern. Women cannot afford to let their rights be simply dismissed with the statement that "Islam liberated women" and that there is therefore no cause for complaint.

There are progressive voices within American Muslim communities addressing these topics today, though unless one is listening for them, they tend to be drowned out by conservatives. Growing numbers of Muslim women are interpreting the Qur'an, and their writings and lectures are having an impact. Muslim women's discussion groups at mosques, as well as in academic and activist settings, are a force for change. The single most important idea associated with all these efforts is that men and women are created equal as believers and that, ultimately, their equality as human beings in the sight of God matters more than any distinctions based on social hierarchy.

I am optimistic that this idea, and its natural consequence of more egalitarian families, communities, and laws, will shape the future of Muslims in the United States. I do not expect it will happen overnight, nor without significant conflict, but I do believe it is the only way for Muslims to truly live out the Divine command for men and women to be protectors of one another.

Kecia Ali is the senior research analyst responsible for Islam with the Feminist Sexual Ethics project at Brandeis University. Her research focuses on marriage and spousal rights in early Islamic jurisprudence.

BORN IN THE U.S.A.

A JOURNALIST INTERVIEWS AMERICAN *MUSLIMAHS* WHO PROVE
THAT DEVOTION AND WOMEN'S LIBERATION DO MIX.

By Miriam Udel-Lambert

Ilham Hameedduddin, in a loose robe and headscarf, is often mistaken for a foreigner. Although her mother is Indian and her father
Arab-Indian, Hameedduddin was raised in the United States, attended public schools, and is working toward a B.A. at Middlesex
College in New Jersey. Nevertheless, she says, "Neighbors are surprised I can speak English without an accent. They assume I'm
fresh off the boat and I just haven't assimilated yet."

Actually, Hameedduddin doesn't plan to assimilate, at least
not as far as her religion is concerned. As a proud American and
devout Muslim, she is part of a new, "indigenous" American
Muslim generation. Until now, this country's Muslim community
has included several subgroups: immigrants from Arab countries
and the Indian subcontinent, along with American converts of European or African-American descent. Since immigration restrictions were eased in the late 1960s, many Middle Eastern and
South Asian Muslims have come to the States, building a network
of mosques and Islamic schools in major metropolitan centers,
such as Philadelphia and Los Angeles, as well as enclaves in smaller
cities like Dearborn, Michigan, and Syracuse, New York, and in

smaller towns throughout the country. These developments dove-tailed with the growth of the Black Muslim movement, an African-American nationalist religious group founded in Detroit in 1930. Today, a splinter group called the Nation of Islam and led by Louis Farrakhan remains distinct, but the majority of African-American Muslims belong to mainstream Islam.

Now, according to Georgetown Islamic scholar Yvonne Haddad, the children of these disparate immigrants and converts are in college and graduate school. They are intermarrying with one another, engaging each other socially and religiously, and gen-erally fusing their ranks into a single Islamic community. By virtue of the American context in which this community is emerging—with its emphasis on pluralism and acceptance of difference—it of-fers women a more public role as workers, activists, and decision makers than most other Islamic societies. A new kind of American Islam, therefore, is being created in which women can be at once devout and publicly active.

AMERICAN ISLAM OFFERS NEW OPTIONS

The first indication of the openness of American Islam is the way Muslims from different points on the religious and cultural spec-trum describe women's religious and communal activities. No matter how religiously liberal or conservative, and regardless of background, all emphasize that Muslim women are engaging in as vast an array of careers and causes as other American women. Ac-cording to Cynthia Sulaiman, who converted at age twenty-eight after ten years of deliberation and who now operates the Muslim Homeschooling Resources Network out of her home, "We run just like any other religious community. We have mothers who are strictly stay-at-home and very conservative, women who are doc-tors and scientists, and women who publish magazines for other women. It all depends on what individual women feel they can contribute." She points out that while her community includes many female teachers and health care workers, such professions have been traditional fields for women generally.

There are several factors contributing to this new notion of a devout, but liberated, Muslim woman. First, as Muslims of many ethnicities learn to coexist, they have to learn to be open-minded about each other. And people have applied that new tolerance to women as well. Many mosques serve ethnically, racially, and socioeconomically mixed communities. This is especially true of smaller communities, as Sakina Abdul-Malik points out. While she grew up in Philadelphia in a predominantly African-American mosque, her mosque in Syracuse includes Yemeni, Palestinian, and Malaysian families along with American converts.

In marriage, too, there is much mixing among different Muslims in the United States. Many American-born women are married to Pakistani and Bangladeshi men. According to Haddad, there is a growing rate of intermarriage between Arabs and Pakistanis and between Pakistani men and Bangladeshi women. Meanwhile, all of these families are living in America, rearing children who absorb at least some of the American ethos. The movement toward inter-Muslim integration in this country, with its prospects for a more public role for women, seems inexorable. "There is a fear of the unknown on the part of parents who believe the more you have someone like you, the happier the marriage is," concedes Haddad. "They absolutely want their children to marry someone from the same country and social class, but the kids aren't paying attention."

A second indicator that American Islam offers new options to women is that young women have taken on a very visible, vocal role as political activists—something that is less common in many Muslim countries. During an election in Hameedduddin's community, teenage girls manned a booth outside a local mosque during Friday prayers, urging congregation members to register to vote. Some women choose lesser public engagement, but even they are careful to note that their choices are individual and shouldn't be binding for all Muslim women.

Expressing an attitude typical of many American Muslims, Hameedduddin is deeply respectful of her coreligionists abroad. "In Islamic countries," she points out, "women are much more active among themselves. The 'behind-the-scenes' roles are not lesser roles," she asserts. If American Muslim women play a more visible role, it is in the service of achieving their goals. "It's true that women and especially the American youth are much more aggressive in their approach. We've learned new ways to make our voices heard, be active in the community, and draw positive attention to our community. American Muslim women are more assertive than Arab ones because that is simply how American society is set up."

As women become more vocal—more American—they are not straying from their religion, however. Instead, women have brought American activism to their religion. Both scholars and practitioners of the religion are impressed with the enthusiasm that converts often exhibit upon joining the community. Haddad, who has studied American Muslims extensively, notes that female converts take a lot of initiative in establishing religious schools because they are eager for their children to receive a proper Islamic education. Furthermore, they tend to serve as liaisons with non-Muslims because "they feel themselves to be ambassadors to the larger American society."

Moreover, novices may insert vigor into their religious communities. Hameedduddin contrasts those who are born into Islam and "take it for granted" with a young woman who converted a year-and-a-half ago and is very good at organizing events in the mosque. "I think she has brought energy from outside the religion," Hameedduddin notes. "People like her are more grateful they found Islam."

Sulaiman sees the high-profile contributions of converts as a function of practical know-how in dealing with American institutions and systems rather than as a manifestation of religious passion. Most of the organizing work in her community in eastern Massachusetts is done by converts like herself, says Sulaiman, but this is only natural. "I'm in my native country," she points out, "and I don't expect immigrants to know what to do in my country. It would be really presumptuous to walk into a country and say, 'Okay, you have to do this and this.'" Abdul-Malik, an African-American woman who grew up Muslim in Philadelphia, echoes her close friend Sulaiman: "Women from overseas are often homebound, into doing things just with their families. Those born on this coast are used to doing things in a community."

Muslim Web sites teem with first-person accounts of "Why I Became Muslim." Many of the authors are female, as women are among the fastest-growing segments of the Muslim community, according to Ibrahim Hooper of the Council for American-Islamic Relations. It is women, therefore, who are helping speed the path to the new American type of Islam.

LIBERATION, NOT OPPRESSION

Though American Muslim women are comfortable with their roles, many non-Muslim women are mystified by Islam's appeal. They know that Islam permits polygamy (a controversial practice, though) and, as it is interpreted in several countries, grossly limits women's educational and career choices as well as their freedom of movement and dress.

These restrictions, however, are only part of the picture—and a secondary part for the Western women who are choosing the religion. In her cogent analysis, *Women and Gender in Islam*, Egyptian-born scholar Leila Ahmed argues that in matters concerning women, there is a dichotomy between the practice of Islam as codified by the legal tradition and the egalitarian vision portrayed by the Qur'an. She writes, "The unmistakable presence of an ethical egalitarianism explains why Muslim women frequently insist, often inexplicably to non-Muslims, that Islam is not sexist. They hear and read in its sacred text, justly and legitimately, a different message from that heard by the makers and enforcers of orthodox, androcentric Islam." When interpreted directly from the text—rather than when observed in its most restrictive application—Islam may be understood as egalitarian.

While many Western women consider certain Muslim practices oppressive, others interpret them as liberating. Some women, for example, argue that embracing Muslim norms of modesty releases them from the sexual current underlying many everyday interactions. "Islam offers an alternative to a sexually charged and sexually exploitative society," Hooper asserts. "Islam allows women to disengage from an environment that values them only for their sexuality and physical appearance and seeks to eliminate sexuality from nonsexual relationships. If a woman goes to the butcher shop, she doesn't need to look pretty to get meat."

As Muslims negotiate their relationship with American culture—and with Muslims of other ethnicities in the United States—a window has opened for a renegotiated role for women. Taking advantage of that opportunity, women may seek the most egalitarian interpretation of the Qur'an while preserving the traditions they find meaningful. This new role for women may strengthen both women's options and American Islam itself.

Miriam Udel-Lambert is a writer living in New York City.

MUHAMMAD'S LEGACY
FOR WOMEN

A PROFESSOR CONTRASTS HER OWN FAMILY'S HIGH REGARD FOR WOMEN
WITH THE OPPRESSIVE TENDENCIES OF SOME MUSLIMS TODAY.

By Leila Dabbagh

I was born into a Muslim family and learned about Islam and the respect accorded women from the behavior of the men around me. I especially treasure my memories of my maternal grandfather. He was always waiting at the door when I came home from school to ask me what I had learned that day and marvel at my progress. He cried with joy when I graduated high school. He held and gazed at my diploma for hours afterwards. A devout Muslim, he loved the fact that his granddaughter was getting an education.

My father's family had many imams, teachers, and scholars of Islam. Learning for both men and women was held in high esteem. The number of college graduates among the women in my family has increased with each generation. From my father's behavior and that of his uncles, I saw how natural it was for men and women to gather socially in the same room and converse about family and life. My great-uncles shook my mother's hand and smiled when they greeted her. They were devout Muslim men from Mecca, but many young Muslims today would consider such behavior sacrilege.

My fondest memory of my great-uncle Saleh is the way in which he frequently addressed his wife with such poetic language; he flirted with her, joked with her, and sang to her without being self-conscious that there were other people around. He carried her tea trays and helped her wash and clean and tidy up.

My ancestors faithfully practiced the five pillars of Islam without losing sight of the fundamental requirements of everyday civil and compassionate living. Their love, devotion, and deep respect for their wives is unlike any of the characterizations portrayed by "fundamental" misogynistic Muslim men of today. Those were men who lived their lives to parallel that of the Prophet Muhammad in kindness, affection, gentleness, generosity, and respect toward women.

So it grieves me greatly to see men who describe themselves as Muslims transgressing against women in the name of Islam. The Taliban, and others like them, have had extremely deficient schooling in Islam. The Prophet Muhammad championed the movement that gave women protective rights and respect in a culture that treated them as inferior. He made a deliberate move toward eliminating the practice of female infanticide. He considered women as equals and freely supported their independent voice. He encouraged their debates and asked for their opinions. He had no qualms about men seeking advice from wives or daughters. He had no qualms about his wives and daughters joining in conversation to debate political and social issues in the company of other men. I wonder, in the face of such a legacy, how some Muslims justify their intolerance for women's education, independence, and free speech, and how violence and misogynistic practices against women have come to be associated with Islam today.

The issue of polygamy is often raised as an example of women's lower status in Islam. The West, especially the United States, seems singularly fascinated by this matter. In reality, the single verse in the Qur'an that seems to permit polygamy also prohibits it on the grounds that no man would ever be able to fairly balance the strings of his purse and his heart equally between two or more women. The Prophet Muhammad was married monogamously to his first wife, Khadija, for twenty years. When she died, he cried and mourned deeply for her. The multiple marriages in which he engaged afterward were acts of kindness to his community: Many of the women he married were either orphaned or widowed and had no kin to safeguard them from the difficulties that awaited them physically and socially in the Arabian desert. Some he married for political purposes—to unite tribes and make peace. Men who practice polygamy today do not come near the standard of behavior that the Prophet worked so hard to establish for women fourteen centuries ago.

When the Prophet Muhammad was asked by one of his followers, "What is religion?" his response was not related to the five pillars of Islam. He answered instead, "Religion is one's regard and conduct towards others." What sets a faithful believer apart from a merely practicing one is his (or her) regard and conduct toward women, men, children, and other living things. My hope is that Muslims who have strayed from the code of conduct established by the Prophet Muhammad return to it and never lose sight of its nobility.

Leila Dabbagh was born in Jeddah, Saudi Arabia. She is currently a professor of public health and is developing a Hajj (pilgrimage) project that aims to enable and educate service providers and pilgrims from more than one hundred countries to reduce disease and accident rates during the annual journey to Mecca.

WHY EVERY MOSQUE
SHOULD BE WOMAN-FRIENDLY

THERE IS NO EXCUSE FOR BARRING WOMEN FROM PLACES OF PRAYER,
SAYS A MUSLIM POET AND AUTHOR.

By *Saraji Umm Zaid*

> *"Do not stop the maidservants of Allah from going
> to the mosques of Allah."*
> —*Muwatta of Imam Malik*

I once took a trip with my family to the state of Colorado. I was
looking forward to visiting a different Muslim community. To my
great dismay, when we went to attend a Friday congregational
prayer, we were told that no women pray in that mosque and that
I would be unable to pray there. With my children and non-
Muslim mother in tow, I went off to a park while my husband
prayed. I felt humiliated and angry, and I was embarrassed for the
ummah (community) that my mother should have to see Muslims
barring me from a house of God for no reason other than my
gender. Nothing like reinforcing negative stereotypes, is there?
Later, the brothers there told my husband that it was nothing
against me, there just "wasn't room" for women in this mosque.

A few years ago, I visited a mosque in New York, intending
to perform the afternoon prayer while I was out shopping for

things for my new home with my daughter and a friend. Instead, my friend and I were greeted at the door by a very angry teenager, who railed at us to return to our homes, that women have no place in the mosque, and that we were a *fitna* (a trial, calamity, or affliction) upon the brothers who were there. Mind you, we were a group consisting of a small child, a sister in *hijab* (head-covering), and a sister in *niqab* (face veil). If a small child and two sisters in *hijab* are a *fitna* upon these men, then whatever do they do as they walk around New York City and encounter women who cover nothing more than what they are legally required to cover? As we were leaving, one of the brothers caught up to us and apologized for the incident. Then he said, "It's not that women aren't allowed, just that there isn't any room for you in this mosque."

Maybe it's just me, but the "we don't have room for you" excuse is getting old. I visited a mosque in Monterey, California, that was about the size of my living room. If any mosque had a valid reason to use this excuse it was this place. The brothers here, however, had the foresight to curtain off a corner in the back for women. If no women showed up, they would keep the curtain drawn to the side, and there would be more room for men. If a sister or two did show up, they would close the curtain, and the men would have to make do with the space they had left.

Yes, some mosques are very small, but to use that as an excuse to bar women from praying there is unacceptable. Because the Prophet Muhammad specifically forbade keeping women from the mosque, no one is going to come right out and say that they bar women from entering. "We don't have room" becomes code for "We don't want you here. Go home." If people were really interested in keeping with the Prophet's practice, they should make sure that their mosque doesn't aid them in violating his command.

People in these communities who speak out against this injustice are often labeled "troublemakers." When I wrote a letter to that New York mosque, giving reasons from Qur'an, Sunnah, and the writings of our esteemed scholars as to why it is forbidden to block women from the mosque, I was labeled a "radical feminist."

Is antifeminism so ingrained in our community now that any speech for the rights of women should be dismissed, even when that speech comes directly from Allah and his messenger?

Besides the inconvenience such mosques pose to women who are traveling, or working, or in some other way unable to pray at home or at a local mosque, these mosques also detract from the community as a whole. A multitude of viewpoints, ideas, and energy have been eliminated. More than 50 percent of the local community becomes invisible and excluded. Actually, more than 50 percent because when a mosque excludes women, it often excludes young children as well. Is this the public face of our *da'wa* (the invitation to Islam)? A face that is exclusively male? How can we tell non-Muslim women that Islam is a sheltering place for them if we show them a community in which women are virtually invisible?

When you ensure that women are included in the mosque, you are ensuring that the entire community has access to the teachings of Islam. You are showing others that Islam does not stand for the exclusion of women and children, that Islam is not a "man's religion." You are showing others that a woman can be modest, can be religious, and can still participate in community life. You are showing the next generation of Muslims that cultural ideas about excluding women and keeping them in the home are not from Islam. And you are following the teachings and example of our beloved Prophet. It is time for us to undo the damage done to our communities by pre-Islamic cultural ideas about "women's place." It is time for us to erase the misconceptions and misunderstandings of the religion that many still cling to. The only way that we can be sure that the next generation understands Islam as it was truly taught by the Prophet is to be sure that women and children are fully included in the mosque.

Saraji Umm Zaid is a freelance writer whose articles have appeared in Q-News: The Muslim Magazine and Azizah magazine. She won the first annual Andalusia Prize for Short Fiction in 2000 for her story "Making Maqlooba" and is a featured poet at www.muslimpoet.com. She lives in New York City and works with a nonprofit Islamic group promoting traditional and classical knowledge.

ABUSE, POLYGAMY, EXCLUSION: THREE STORIES OF AMERICAN MUSLIM WOMEN

AN ATTORNEY CHALLENGES THE MUSLIM COMMUNITY
TO ACKNOWLEDGE—AND FIGHT—ATTITUDES THAT DEMEAN WOMEN.

By Samer Hathout

Women in the United States often face gender-based discrimination. While this discrimination may not be as overt as in other parts of the world or may take different forms, it does exist.

American Muslim women face these and many additional hurdles. For instance, a woman who wears *hijab*, the traditional head-covering, is often taunted at work and on the street, and the careers of these women are jeopardized. Women who wear *hijab* in the United States are targets—they are obviously Muslim to others and thus bear the brunt of the ignorance about Islam. They face sexual harassment, and often their physical safety is at risk.

In addition, Muslim women often face discrimination from their own Muslim communities, stemming primarily from ignorance about Islam and the importation of cultural attitudes that demean women. Islam is often interpreted in ways that are sexist and not true to the core teachings of equality in the Qur'an and the model provided by the Prophet Muhammad. Qur'an and *ha-*

111

dith (the traditional sayings of the Prophet Muhammad) are often taken out of context and used to justify certain behavior.

In America, Muslim immigrants face a host of problems. There is a growing hostility toward immigrants, and they are often erroneously blamed for social and economic problems and are harassed because of that. African-American Muslims face additional hurdles—racism, discrimination, segregation, and the vestiges of slavery. Add religious discrimination and gender discrimination, and you have a glimpse of the challenges American Muslim women face.

Because Muslims are a minority in the United States attempting to portray a truer, more positive image of Islam, they are sometimes reluctant to address the problems faced by Muslim women for fear that this information will be used against us. But the ironic part is that everyone knows the problems we face. And unfortunately, the media is quick to inform us and others of the more serious forms of this abusive discrimination. I would therefore like to recognize some of the problems that we as American Muslim women face and give voice to our sisters who have suffered wrongly in the name of Islam.

WOMEN'S STORIES

Some of the most serious problems that we face include domestic violence, abuse of divorce and child custody laws, abuse of the polygamy system, and isolation and exclusion from various aspects of Muslim life. Unfortunately, there is no central database of reported abuse and no accurate sense of its frequency. Further research is desperately needed. To illustrate both the depth of the problems and the specific suffering of American Muslim women today, I have provided a few anecdotal cases—these are true stories compiled from Muslim community leaders, social workers, psychologists, lawyers, and doctors. I have changed the names and personal details of the women in the stories to protect their identities. I also obtained information from Sistersnet, an e-mail network of Muslim women in the United States and other countries. These cases may not be experienced by a majority of American Muslim women, but they nevertheless present serious issues that must be addressed.

Mariam

Mariam was married for several years to a man named Ali, who abused her both verbally and physically. Mariam was often beaten by her husband. When Mariam did attempt to speak with her local Muslim community leader, she was made to feel that the abuse was her fault—if she were a better wife, Ali would not have to beat her. She was also told not to discuss her marital problems with other people and that it was important for her to stay married at all costs to preserve the family. Ali would quote the Qur'an and *hadith* to justify his abuse.

Finally, Mariam couldn't stand it any more. She feared for her life. She left her home and her husband and sought refuge in a local battered women's shelter. There she received the assistance that she needed to put her life back together. Ali was convicted in U.S. court for spousal battery. But when Mariam appeared at Muslim functions, she was shunned; the Muslim community wanted nothing to do with her. She was viewed as a woman who had left her husband for no reason. Ali, on the other hand, was viewed as the victim of a broken marriage and of the United States criminal justice system. He was greeted by the Muslim community with open arms. Mariam found no support from the Muslim community and eventually stopped attending Muslim functions.

Mariam's story is unfortunately not an uncommon one. Victims of domestic violence have little support from the Muslim community, and the support they do receive, while well-intentioned, is often unorganized and ineffectual. The lives of domestic violence victims are often in danger, and their only recourse is to turn to non-Muslim organizations that are prepared to deal with this issue.

Khadija and Fatima

The story of Khadija and Fatima shows the abuses of the polygamy system in Islam. Khadija married Omar under the laws of the state in which he lived and under Islamic law. Omar later took a second wife, Fatima. But Omar and Fatima could not get married under U.S. law because he was already married. So Omar married Fatima under a—supposed—Islamic tradition that includes simply a marriage proposal and an acceptance of that proposal in front of witnesses. Fatima, the second wife, who was a convert to Islam, learned Islam mostly from Omar, and he convinced her that they did not need to be married under U.S. law. He told her that Islam would sufficiently protect her rights. While this is true theoretically, there is no framework in the United States to enforce it.

Omar had children with both of his wives. Both marriages failed. Khadija and Omar divorced, and Omar refused to pay any support to Khadija or their children. Omar was obligated under Islamic law to do these things, but he refused. Khadija, however, could take Omar to court and get child support and alimony under the laws of the United States.

Fatima, on the other hand, had no recourse because she was not legally married in the eyes of the U.S. courts. Omar shirked his responsibilities under Islamic law and didn't give her or their children financial support. There was no legal institution compelling Omar to comply with Islamic law.

Iman

Iman is a university student and an activist who was elected to her student senate. She has formed coalitions with other student groups to do relief work for Bosnia, Palestine, and Chechnya. She wants to organize similar relief efforts in her local mosque and in other mosques in the area so that she can reach a larger Muslim population. But when she tries to post flyers and information in her mosque, she can't get to the men's section. She can reach the women's section, but few women attend because the facilities are less than adequate. Iman does not have a brother, father, or husband to access the men's side for her. When she asks men at the mosque for help in disseminating information, she is often ignored. Occasionally she gets some help, but the next time she can't find the same person and has to go through the same process again and again.

Iman isn't allowed to make an announcement after the Friday prayer because she is a woman. She is told that she cannot run for the board of the mosque because she is a woman. Instead, she is invited to join the women's committee and organize Eid carnivals for the children and prepare *iftar* (breakfast) during Ramadan. Iman is extremely frustrated. As an activist, she has work she cares about doing. So she eventually stops going to the mosque because she can do more through the non-Muslim human rights groups at her university.

As Iman's story shows, Muslim-American women are regularly excluded from leadership positions in our mosques and in our Islamic centers. We are allowed to participate only in certain areas—preparing food, organizing Eid festivities, and events of that sort. Women are absent from educational or spiritual roles, except when they are teaching other women or children. Women with Islamic knowledge and expertise are not allowed to explain the Qur'an to the congregation or give lessons in Islamic law. Gender segregation is imposed in most American mosques and results in unfair and unequal access to space and facilities. Women are often put in areas with poor sound systems, or none at all, or noisy makeshift childcare areas. They are stuck in back rooms next to the bathrooms, and wherever they are put—even if it's a great facility—they still can't interact with the speaker and ask questions and have their voices heard.

American Muslim women are not just excluded from leadership positions in our communities but also even excluded from mosques completely. This exclusion can be overt, where we are told "this is a men's mosque," or it can be subtle, where the facilities provided are so inadequate and the treatment is so horrendous that no reasonable woman would go back. All of this exclusion has no basis in the teachings of Islam.

These are just a few of the abuses suffered by Muslim women in America. Again, we raise these issues not because we are against Islam, but because we—as Muslims—need to deal with the problems. It is not enough to say that Islam is a great religion. We need to prove it with our actions.

As Muslims, it is our duty to fight against every form of oppression, whatever form it takes, by whatever means we can, and we cannot fight oppression if we do not acknowledge that it exists.

Samer Hathout is the founding president of the Muslim Women's League and is the vice chairperson of the Muslim Public Affairs Council in Los Angeles. A recipient of the Miller Johnson Equal Justice Award, she traveled with the Muslim Women's League to Croatia to investigate the status of Bosnian refugees. Currently, she works as a criminal prosecutor in Los Angeles.

HALAL, HARAM,
AND *SEX AND THE CITY*

A YOUNG MUSLIM LAWYER ON THE AMERICAN DATING SCENE.

By Asma Gull Hasan

When I was in middle school, I attended the wedding of a family friend's son. The event seemed overwhelming, with Pakistani-Americans like my family—dads who were doctors and moms dressed in glittery, gaudy Pakistani dress. The groom was Pakistani, but his bride was not. She was white and non-Muslim. The fabric of her Pakistani wedding dress was a rich orange color that made her skin seem even whiter and her hair even more red. She complained about how itchy her blouse was. My sister noted later to me that she had it on inside out, so all the embroidery was on the inside, scratching her skin. But problems with her bridal outfit intrigued me less than the fact that she was a white woman marrying a man of Pakistani descent. How did these two meet? I wanted to ask my sister, "Did their parents arrange their marriage?"

They had probably met at work and dated each other. I couldn't admit this to my teenage self because I knew that Muslims did not date. We had arranged marriages, just like my mom and dad did.

Well, not really. In Islamic countries, parents have the support of the community in finding spouses for their children. Word

117

of mouth, relatives, and a social schedule and circuit make arranging marriages easier. In the United States, parents are isolated
from these networks.

Further, most Muslims now push their daughters to achieve
in academics and in a career. For Muslim immigrants, the opportunities for their daughters are hard to resist. For indigenous,
mostly African-American Muslims, the civil rights era gave their
children access to educational opportunities that were previously
closed to them. A trade-off has been made, though. The more educated the daughter, the less comfortable a parent feels arranging
her marriage. My parents could have locked me up at home and
picked my husband for me. But then how could I have gone to college? In fact, the very same parents who had marriages arranged
for them are now reluctant to do the same for their own children.

So how are young American Muslims supposed to meet and
marry each other, especially when Islamic religious or cultural
events are often segregated by gender? Young American Muslims
have come up with creative solutions to dating. They fall into
roughly three categories. The first group are "strict Muslims" who
date *halal* (Islamically permissible). The second group I call "Eid
Muslims" because many are not strict in practice and attend
mosques only on holidays. While technically they are dating *haram*
(unlawfully), without chaperones, they're keeping physical inti-
macy to a minimum and parental involvement at a maximum. The
third group dates *Sex and the City*–style (definitely *haram*), openly
and freely leading a non-Islamic lifestyle, having premarital sex,
sometimes in a series of monogamous relationships.

This last group consists mostly of Muslim men who date
non-Muslim women. These non-Muslim women sometimes convert to Islam and marry their Muslim boyfriends. But some are un-
ceremoniously dumped when a *halal* marriage is arranged by the
man's parents. The woman's family is naturally upset at how she
has been treated, resulting in a misconception that Muslim men

treat women poorly. Ironically, a Muslim man can date freely without risking his standing in the community, while a Muslim woman with the same dating pattern would not only acquire a bad reputation but also risk losing a good arranged marriage proposal. This double standard and poor treatment of women is not endorsed by Islam but by a general patriarchy that pervades many world cultures, including America.

Upon getting serious with a woman they're dating, though, some of these *Sex and the City* men suddenly reassert their strict Wahhabi upbringing. They insist that their girlfriends, with whom they once openly had sex, will now have to wear a cover and stay at home, and that their dating relationship was *haram*. A friend of mine who had such an experience broke off the engagement with the Muslim man but retained her commitment to Islam. She said many of her friends were surprised that she didn't return to the party-girl lifestyle once her Muslim fiancé was out of the picture. But she told me she is now committed to waiting to have sex again until she marries.

My friend wants to engage in *halal* dating—a practice gaining much popularity in the American Muslim community both among strict Muslims and Eid Muslims. *Halal* dating is the first cousin of arranged marriage, with young people finding their own mates— within the guidelines of Islam—instead of their parents arranging marriages for them. Because the Qur'an advocates equality between the sexes, it does not permit premarital sex—since all the negative consequences fall upon the woman, including pregnancy, the social stigma, and the raising of the child. Premarital sex is also forbidden for other reasons, including learning to discipline oneself and practice self-control. Under Islam, when a man has sex with a woman to whom he is not married, he is being disrespectful of her, regardless of whether she is consensually participating. So young Muslims who engage in *halal* dating seek a commitment first and are vigilant about staying true to their religion.

For both strict and Eid Muslims, couples are often introduced to each other, either by parents or friends. They spend time
talking on the phone or over the Internet and even going on dates,
though for strict Muslims, a chaperone is always present. Once
they have decided they like each other, the couple is married
under Islamic law by signing a marriage contract. This event, called
the *nikah*, is as binding as a marriage. The couple, however, is seen
as engaged in most Islamic cultures and in American Islamic culture. The signing of the agreement allows them to spend more
time together. Strict Muslims still have a chaperone present and
the couple do not even hold hands.

In *halal* dating, a clear understanding exists between the man
and the woman that they are committed to marrying each other.
They view the other as a life partner, not a hot prom date. Eventually they will obtain a marriage license and marry in a ceremony
to which they invite their friends and family.

Sometimes, though, the engagement is ended, but because
the couple was *halal*, no stigma attaches to them. Many Muslims
marry non-Muslims who convert as a result of *halal* dating. Another friend of mine, a divorced non-Muslim, met a Muslim of
Pakistani descent in her medical school class. They dated *halal* and
married. He even adopted her daughter from a previous marriage.

Islamic law itself can be fluid in matters of the heart, depending on who is wielding the gavel. Many non-Muslims see
Islam as a gigantic, static monolith, when in fact, Islam can be very
dynamic. Shi'ite Muslims, for instance, sometimes use the device
of *mut'a* to facilitate dating. A *mut'a* is a temporary marriage recognized under Shi'ite practice. An agreement, oral or written, is
created between the man and woman, securing for the woman
certain rights in the event of pregnancy or at the termination of
the marriage. I once heard of a young Muslim couple living together before their formal wedding ceremony. Their parents could
not bear their children living together unmarried so they secured

a *mut'a fatwa* (an Islamic legal ruling that a temporary marriage may take place) for them. Their living together was then *halal*.

As for me, I look at it this way: Whether the use of *mut'a* is right or wrong, whether *halal* dating is indeed *halal* isn't the issue. In the end, we Muslims believe that God will decide, as he is the final judge of us all.

Asma Gull Hasan, the author of American Muslims: The New Generation, *thinks* halal *meat and* halal *dating taste better. She is not sure whether she will have an arranged marriage. To read excerpts of her book, please visit www.asmahasan.com.*

"YOU SEEM SO INTELLIGENT. WHY ARE YOU A MUSLIM?"

A WOMAN WHO SEEMED TO "HAVE IT ALL" RECOUNTS HER SPIRITUAL VOYAGE TO ISLAM.

By Halima Touré

A few years after I embraced Islam, a woman I worked for said to me, "You seem so intelligent. Why are you a Muslim?" I responded, "Because Islam appealed to my head as well as to my heart."

If anyone had told me a year before I became a Muslim that my head and heart would be open to Islam, my response would have been, "You're out of your mind!" So how did I come to this point in my life?

On the outside, I had a good life. As a beneficiary of the civil rights movement, I became the first black editor at *Redbook* magazine in the mid-1960s. Then I freelanced for magazines and did research for television. I had a rich social and professional network. I believed, along with my friends and colleagues, that we could help make a positive change in America. It was the time of "Say it loud: I'm black and I'm proud." My Afro hairstyle and my support for the black arts movement expressed my black pride. The knowledge of Africa's great past awakened my African identity. My family was proud and supportive of my accomplishments. I'd made it.

On the inside, though, a creeping emptiness had begun to spread. I'd joined freedom rides, picket lines, and boycotts with the Congress of Racial Equality. I had volunteered with the National Urban League. But the bullets that killed John F. Kennedy, Robert Kennedy, Malcolm X, and Martin Luther King Jr. each killed a bit of my spirit and hope. Cynicism began to take root.

Meanwhile, I had drifted away from organized religion and settled on the middle ground of agnosticism. The death of a twenty-four-year-old relative left me angry and confused that God would take such a nice guy when so many bad people were creating mayhem. Neither my childhood beliefs nor my adult agnosticism could comfort or satisfy me.

FINDING ANSWERS

The deep questions of life that periodically rise in us all began to surface: If I'd "made it," why did I feel so empty? Material goods, career, family, and friends alone did not fill my inner space. Is life just a free fall from birth to death? Is this all there is? Why am I here? I became hungry for meaning.

Then I met the man who would become my husband and the father of my child. He was a Muslim. He talked of our ancestors' African Islamic identity, along with his dream of a new future for people of African descent. He emphasized how our African past was linked to Islam in empires like Songhai and Mali and in renowned centers of learning like Timbuktu.

I read literature about the basic tenets of Islam. Several were similar to Christianity, although there were fundamental differences. The concept of unity (*tawhid*—the interconnectedness of all things) touched a deep chord in me. I saw how all parts of me— mind, body, spirit—connected to my total environment. This, for me, was profound.

At Friday services in the mosque, the imam, an African-American who had studied Islam at al-Azhar University in Egypt, described Islam as a scientific way of life bound by God's spiritual, physical, and social laws. He believed it was just the medicine needed to uplift humanity, but especially for African-Americans suffering the after-effects of slavery.

I was impressed by the focus on family and by the bonds of brotherhood and sisterhood. Given the popular perception of the absentee African-American father, I was particularly impressed by seeing Muslim men talking to and laughing with young children, even holding infants. The women drew me into their circle and freely answered my questions.

I had met Betty Shabazz, the late widow of El-Hajj Malik El-Shabazz (Malcolm X), when I was helping to edit a book about her husband. When she learned of my engagement, she extolled for me the benefits of being married to a Muslim man. In addition to their focus on family and responsibility, those men were sincere in practicing the faith and believed it was their duty to protect and support their wives and treat them with love and respect. She also pointed out that the ideal of Islam was free of racism and classism.

An *'id āl-fitr* prayer service at the Islamic Center revealed the international character of Islam. In contrast to the racial separation of the United States on Sunday mornings, the colorful tapestry of humanity worshiping together impressed me as just what Allah intended. With the diversity was the unity—black, brown, yellow, and white prostrating themselves before their Creator, reciting the same prayers in the same tongue and intoning in unison, "*Allahu Akbar*" (God is greatest).

THE WORK BEGINS

On the evening that I sat in *hijab* (headscarf) on the carpet in front of the imam, ready to make my *shahada* (profession of faith), I was convinced that I needed Islam for me and not just to please my future husband. Before witnesses, I professed that there is no God but God (Allah), and that Muhammad is his prophet and messenger. Also, I professed belief in Allah's angels, in the Books of Allah, in Allah's prophets, and in life after death. Then the imam said, "You've taken the first step toward becoming a Muslim. Now the work begins."

That work is never-ending. It began with studying—learning what is *halal* (lawful) and *haram* (prohibited), and why. It continues with trying to incorporate its principles into all aspects of my world. I gave away the clothes of my old life, covered my hair, and made ankle- and wrist-length garments that both cover and conceal. The duty-free alcohol went down the toilet; the cigarettes went into the garbage. I scrutinized food labels to avoid *haram* ingredients. I learned the cleansing ritual before prayers, and I learned the prayers themselves. Gradually, I changed my work schedule in order to attend Friday services. The Islamic holy days replaced the holidays of my old tradition.

These outward changes were traumatic enough. My inward shifts, however, were, and continue to be, the most astonishing. For one, I was unaware of the extent of my arrogance and ignorance until I had to bow down to Allah in prayer. My credo had been, "I am the master of my fate! I am the captain of my soul!"

Yes, a measure of free will exists to make choices. What I came to understand, though, is that the great "I" played no part in providing the essentials of life that I took for granted: the air we breathe, the rain that nourishes our food plants, the sun that fuels life-sustaining processes. So shouldn't we humble ourselves to this powerful and generous creator? Could there be a more appropriate gesture of reverence?

Another big shift came five years after I embraced Islam. My father died suddenly of a massive stroke. I was grief stricken, but my behavior and attitude were different from what I had displayed ten years earlier when my young relative died. True, my father was older, but sixty-two is not so old. What was different was me.

What Muslims say on this occasion had real meaning: "We all come from Allah and to him we shall return." I could express my gratitude to Allah for long talks I'd had with my father over the previous year, evidence of a closeness we'd experienced that hadn't existed since I was a child. And despite my pain, I could be grateful that Allah took him swiftly.

Albert Einstein once said, "A problem cannot be solved on the same level of consciousness at which it was created." The hopelessness, cynicism, anxiety, rage, and despair that mark contemporary life—symptoms of an individual's and a society's loss of meaning—threatened to consume me. But on that day nearly thirty years ago, I opened a door to become something else, and I am still "becoming."

I could not comprehend how seeing life through the lens of an Islamic consciousness would change me. One friend was turned off by my zeal, screaming, "Give me a break!" Time and experience have since mellowed me.

My *hijab* and peaceful demeanor surprised another friend who saw me about eight years after my *shahada*. He remarked, "It suits you!"

Yes, it does suit me, and I have yet to feel empty again.

Halima Touré is a writer and a lecturer in the Department of Language and Cognition at Hostos Community College in the Bronx.

THE AFRICAN-AMERICAN
EXPERIENCE

As Precious Rasheeda Muhammad reminds us in her essay, Islam in America did not begin in the twentieth century but much earlier, with a centuries-long chapter, brutally erased, in which hundreds of thousands of African Muslims were enslaved in the Americas beginning in the 1600s. What remains of their example, and the courage it bespeaks, still inspires African-American Muslims today.

In contemporary times, the African-American experience with Islam dates back at least to the 1930s, with the emergence of Elijah Muhammad's Nation of Islam. Professor Akbar Muhammad (a son of Elijah Muhammad) remarks in his essay, "African-American, Muslim, and Loyal to the U.S.," that "as converts to Islam and descendants of converts, Muslim African-Americans are usually viewed by their brethren and others as less knowledgeable about Islam." Since September 11, however, and with the advent of punitive and quasi-race-based federal legislation to "root out terrorists in our midst," African-American Muslims turn out to be *experts* in being Muslims after all.

No group has more experience, more community savvy, or more institutional readiness to redress the inequities of racial profiling and incarceration without evidence than they do: Being singled out for special treatment is nothing new to black Americans. In this vein, F. Thaufeer al-Deen suggests, in "Prison and the

Struggle for Dignity," that Arabs, South Asians, and other immi-grant Muslims might now have cause to change their view of African-Americans and Islam: "To what example will these Mus-lims now turn to escape hatred, detention, imprisonment, alien-ation? Perhaps it will be the earlier example, an example about which they are only dimly aware—the example of African-American Muslims."

Of course, Americans of all colors have been turning for years to one African-American Muslim as a stirring example of what it means to be an effective human being. Deborah Caldwell's essay on Muhammad Ali reminds us that being a Muslim can, lit-erally, mean being The Greatest.

"OH, ALLAH, OPERATE ON US!" ISLAM AND THE LEGACY OF AMERICAN SLAVERY

A YOUNG SCHOLAR ON THE IMPACT OF ISLAM ON BLACK AMERICANS' LIBERATION.

By Precious Rasheeda Muhammad

Indelibly etched on the soul of America is the suffering of the African-American people through what is arguably the most brutal system of racism and slavery the world has known. What havoc the images of black bodies hanging from trees, little girls firebombed while playing in church, eyes gouged out for trying to read, and children bred through serial rape of slave girls wreak on the human mind. Slavery, and the severity of the racism it spawned, was an abomination that disconnected millions of Africans from their heritage, leaving them mentally imprisoned and ill equipped to stand upright as functioning members of society. But Islam operated on the mentally imprisoned souls of many of their progeny lost in the wilderness of America and raised their consciousness to the highest status of slave servants of God alone. In their suffering and triumph are lessons to be learned for all who have the courage to listen.

When and where Islam enters into this story begins centuries ago with the Prophet Muhammad as the first antiracist pioneer in

Islam and continues from Bilal ibn Rabah to the refuge of the Muslims in Abyssinia to slavery in America to the growth of Islam in the African-American community to the post-September 11 backlash that thrust Islam and Muslims into the center of the American consciousness. As a result of September 11, immigrant Muslims are seeking wisdom from the struggle of African-American Muslims. For these are a people who understand what it is like to become the hate that hate produced. And these are a people who have taken Islam and used it as an antidote instead of a poison. As one South Asian-American Muslim student asked, "Have immigrant Muslims ever produced a figure like Malik El-Shabazz (Malcolm X) or Muhammad Ali? No Muslim subgroup understands the political process better than the indigenous African-Americans, and no group has more experience as an oppressed minority than they."

There is no god but God! This is the revolutionary message, revealed to the heart of the Prophet Muhammad, that raised up a most ignorant, racist, feuding backward people in his time and lives on in the mission of Islam to unite all of humanity. Islam did not abolish slavery. It paralyzed the stronghold of slavery on the mind by raising all of humankind to the status of slave servants of God alone. In his last sermon, the Prophet said, "All mankind is from Adam and Eve; an Arab has no superiority over a non-Arab nor does a non-Arab have any superiority over an Arab; also a white has no superiority over a black nor has a black any superiority over a white—except by piety and good action." He urged them to listen carefully and to pass on this message to posterity. It is reported that he ordered, "Yield obedience to my successor, although he may be an Abyssinian slave."

SLAVES STRUGGLED HEROICALLY
TO RETAIN THEIR SPIRITUAL ROOTS

Bilal ibn Rabah, an Abyssinian slave, heard the message of Islam, and his soul would not let it go. He defied his master and under extreme torture would only keep crying out subservience to God. *"Ahad, Ahad* [One God]," he proclaimed relentlessly. Abu Bakr, a close companion of the prophet and the first leader of the Muslims after his death, freed Bilal from slavery, and the Prophet Muhammad appointed him as the first *mu'adhdhin,* or one who gives the *adhan,* the Muslim call to prayer. The awe-inspiring voice of this black ex-slave in an Arab land that was not his home resonated with the Arabic call, "God is the Greatest. . . . God is the Greatest. . . . Come to Prayer. . . . Come to Success. . . . There is no god but God." The story of his triumph is a favorite of Muslims around the world. It is no wonder then that the largest organized group of African-American Muslims in America call themselves Bilalians and even produced an internationally circulated paper entitled *Bilalian News,* now the *Muslim Journal.*

The African Negus (king) of Abyssinia answered the call of the Prophet Muhammad to protect Muslims seeking refuge from the Meccans, who abhorred Islam and the new Muslims. The Negus granted refuge to a people oppressed in their own land, not unlike what America has done for immigrants, including Muslims, granting safety and freedom of religion to all. The irony, as pointed out by one young Muslim, is that here in America there are already Muslims—African-American ones. And it is these people of African descent, like the Negus, who welcome Muslims seeking refuge in a land not their own.

Islam flourished in Africa. It is reported that even the Negus became Muslim, and thus a significant number of Africans brought to America were Muslim. And not only were they Muslim, but they were from among the most educated of their people. Many are well-documented as being literate and able to write in Arabic. In 1753, two Muslim slaves petitioned in Arabic for their freedom. And we are all familiar with the story of Kunta Kinte, the Gambian Muslim enslaved in America from Alex Haley's *Roots,* who struggled to maintain his prayers and Arabic writing skills and to pass on what he could of his Islamic legacy. Recent studies have focused on Omar ibn Said, captured from what is now Senegal.

Throughout his enslavement, Said continued his Arabic and Islamic scholarship, writing in Arabic items such as The Lord's Prayer, the *Basmallah*, works on how to pray, Qur'anic phrases, the twenty-third Psalm, and Surah 110 of the Qur'an. So profound was he that his master even gave him an Arabic Bible and the Qur'an. As Sylviane A. Diouf, author of *Servants of Allah: African Muslims Enslaved in the Americas*, states, "The African Muslims may have been, in the Americas, the slaves of Christian masters, but their minds were free. They were the servants of Allah."

Slavery is not the first place that the history of Muslims of African descent in America begins. There were free Muslims who came to the New World and even fought in the Civil War. Records show that as far back as 1312, African Muslims, directed by the brother of Mansa Musa, explored the Americas. Nicholas Said, born Mohammed Ali Ben Said, was an African Muslim enslaved in Africa, Asia, and Europe. He lived on five continents, came to America a free man, and fought in the Civil War from 1863–1865. Said spoke nine languages, including Arabic and Turkish. Though it appears he was a Christian when he died, he dedicated more than half his autobiography, published in the United States in 1873, to recounting his life as a Muslim and his Islamic heritage.

SCARS REMAIN

What separates these free and learned African Muslims in America from the African-American Muslims of today is that they all had a sense of identity, a sense of their language, their family history, and their religion. Though slavery has existed throughout time, there has never been a group of people that were more severed from their culture, their religion, and their life than the African-Americans of today. How does one once considered three-fifths human live, work, give birth, or die? How does a three-fifths human pass on dignity, self-worth, and a sense of "being"? Ultimately, how does a three-fifths human construct a worldview and worship God?

Still, many of them, with only a disconnected understanding of their former names, songs, rituals, and religious ceremonies, have taken up the banner of Islam and carried it through twentieth century America into the twenty-first century. They were led to Islam because of Islam's appeal to humanity. The utter devastation of a people orphaned from their past opened them up to Islam, and it impressed freedom on their hearts while providing a strategy for overcoming what was lost. Islam replaced their lost culture with its obligation that they understand themselves first as members of the human race. An example of this is exemplified in a recent article written by a young scholar activist concerning the Israeli-Palestinian conflict. Hakim Sabree writes, "As Muslims and as African-Americans we have a duty sanctioned by G-d to stand firmly against acts of injustice being perpetrated against any people anywhere in the world. It is impossible to address the concerns of the African-American or black people and not address the concerns of all people because we are all one people, one human family. We are human beings before we are any ethnic group. In fact, we cannot even have an ethnic identity if it isn't first established on the pattern of our human identity."

African-Americans have come to Islam from diverse paths. Theirs is a history deeply imbedded in every Muslim community in America—from popular Islam to Black Nationalism to Sunni to Shi'ite and Sufi—not unlike the diversity of the Muslim world today. Yet, though they came to Islam through different paths and though theirs is a constant struggle and transformation that has led them to study Islam in the farthest corners of the Muslim world and in the ivory towers of America, a common trait seems to bind them together: their dedication to the alleviation of tumult and oppression wherever they find it. As professors, judges, doctors, scholars, activists, students, religious leaders, pioneers, and more, they are active in every aspect of society that is a benefit to humankind.

What every Muslim in America needs to know, then, about

the legacy of Islam in the African-American community is that to ignore it is a loss of a great lesson to all who fight for tolerance, fellowship, and understanding. What Muslim can deny God's hand in taking the lowest of the low, the indigent down in dust, and raising them as Muslim leaders in America? Elitism and prejudice are abhorred in Islam, yet there exists a most intense racism against African-Americans and their rightful place as Muslims in Islamic history. One imam summed this up passionately. Speaking to a predominantly African-American community, he told them that they must not think of themselves as lesser Muslims than their co-religionists because of their race. He reminded them of the Qur'anic teaching that God created humankind, as a favor, different so that they may learn from one another. Upon uttering this, he raised the Qur'an up high and implored, "Which one of these favors of your Lord will you deny?" Still, until September 11, African-Americans were rarely consulted by other Muslims on any issue.

"Oh Allah, operate on us!" Elijah Muhammad cried out to God in one of his last speeches. When Elijah died in 1975, my father, then a member of the Nation of Islam, helped lower his body into the ground. Years ago, when I was writing my undergraduate thesis on the immutable message of Islam and its appeal to the oppressed peoples of African descent in America, I interviewed my father about his experience. He recounted those words to me and told me sadly, "Elijah said that because he was dealing with people who were downtrodden. Through the muck and the mire, he wanted Allah to make us upright people." My father, a part of the Fruit of Islam (FOI), the Nation of Islam's paramilitary unit, stood on honor guard in 1975 as Imam W. Deen Mohammad, a son of Elijah Muhammad, was raised up high on the shoulders of several FOI. This elevation was a celebratory moment marking the commencement of Imam Mohammad's leadership over the Nation of Islam and the impressing upon their hearts the finality of the Prophet Muhammad's revolutionary message, which would finalize their transition into completely upright servants of Allah.

Now is the time when Muslims strap bombs to their bodies because they feel that their only way out of the dehumanization they have suffered is to devastate humanity by stealing the lives of innocent worshippers. Now is the time when suicide bombers, professing to be Muslims, fly planes filled with human bodies into buildings, killing thousands and inciting an entire world to immediately rise up with vicious disgust against Islam. Now is the time for Muslims to learn from a people so tortured that their only saving grace is that they did not become the hate that hate produced.

Herein lies the greatest lesson to be learned from the African-American Muslim legacy, especially potent and telling post-September 11: that as victims of hate, they took Islam and became champions of universal human excellence and compassion for all of humanity. As victims of oppression, they realized long ago that any form of tumult and oppression—not just that of Muslims—is a Muslim issue. They have championed the banner of Islam in this manner long before the voices of other Muslims were heard. From fighting in the Civil War to choosing prison time over service in the Vietnam War to establishing the largest Muslim school system in America to cleaning drugs out of neighborhoods and fishing for souls in overpopulated prisons—their presence in world history and their contribution to making the universal principles of Islam heard over any culture of origin is indelible. The revolutionary message revealed to the Prophet Muhammad was a message for all of humanity. Muslims must never seek safety in the margins where only issues directly affecting them are found.

Precious Rasheeda Muhammad is a third-generation African-American Muslim. Dedicated to tolerance, fellowship, and understanding, she is founder and president of Journal of Islam in America Press, an educational publishing company that publishes a broad range of titles on the growth and development of Islam in America and the Muslim-American experience. A 2001 graduate of Harvard Divinity School with a Masters of Theological Studies, she founded the Islam in America conferences at Harvard.

AFRICAN-AMERICAN, MUSLIM, AND LOYAL TO THE U.S.

A KEY FIGURE IN THE BLACK MUSLIM COMMUNITY SAYS
AFRICAN-AMERICAN MUSLIMS AND THEIR LEADERS HAVE NEW VISIBILITY
AND A NEW OPPORTUNITY TO USE IT WELL.

By Akbar Muhammad, Ph.D.

The catastrophic attacks of September 11, 2001, were the greatest shock the Muslim-American community has ever experienced. For many, a good part of the shock was that the attackers were soon identified as members of the transnational Muslim nation, the *ummah*. How did Muslim African-American leaders respond? What do their responses tell us about their attitudes toward the United States? And what do their responses indicate for the future of Muslims in America?

Although Muslim African-Americans have much in common with their more recent immigrant brethren and their U.S.-born and U.S.-raised offspring, they have a peculiar history. All have backgrounds of social and political oppression. According to many observers, they have love-hate relationships with the former "masters" and their "kind," or, minimally, courteous but somewhat distant relationships. Loyalty to nation-states has been influenced by ethnic-group feelings, their understandings of Islam, and a lack of power to make desired changes in significant areas of life. But

Muslim African-Americans have no vivid memories of national liberation from oppression, nor from slavery.

As converts to Islam and descendants of converts, Muslim African-Americans are usually viewed by their brethren and others as less knowledgeable about Islam. Immigrants and their children enjoy a higher standard of living and education than Muslim African-Americans and seem to be held in higher esteem by European-Americans (i.e., "white" Americans). Muslim associations led by immigrants have become the most listened-to interpreters of Islam in both its "moderate" and "radical" forms. Compared with the times of Elijah Muhammad and Malcolm X (known to Muslims as Malik Shabazz), there has been a remarkable diminution in the national and international position of Muslim African-Americans.

What was the reaction of Muslim African-Americans to the September 11 attacks? While the media, publishing companies, government officials—including President George W. Bush—and an array of Americans attempted to convince the public that Islam is a peaceful faith, some Muslim African-Americans felt compelled to do more. In their defense of Islam and condemnation of the attacks, they explicitly and implicitly expressed loyalty to the United States, respect for other religions, and called for more interfaith cooperation on political, social, and religious matters affecting Americans.

UNIFYING REACTIONS FROM BLACK MUSLIM LEADERS
The leaders of the two most prominent organizations, Minister Louis Farrakhan of the Nation of Islam and Imam W. Deen Mohammad of the much larger Muslim American Society, have considerable influence on the largest number of the estimated 40 percent of the Muslim-American population who are African-American. As the national Muslim leader who seemed to exhibit the most political and religious change since September 2001—

largely unnoticed by the mainstream press—Farrakhan's remarks about the attack and its aftermath deserve closer attention.

In his press statement of September 16, 2001, and on behalf of all Muslims, he implored Allah for "divine guidance" to the American government and people, and said, "No amount of preaching . . . could make the many diverse elements of [American] society come together as brothers and sisters in a unified expression, but tragedy did." He admonished the most powerful nation to be humble, "for only in humility can the proud and powerful heed the Guidance of God. . . . Allah (God) used this tragedy, hopefully, to bring a great nation to Himself. . . . Tragedy was turned into triumph. Tragedy began the spiritual awakening of a great nation and steeled its resolve to overcome the wickedness of those who perpetrated this assault on the United States of America. . . . Those who perpetrated this horrendous act have lost their humanity and . . . become like wild beasts with only one thought in mind, to devour their prey."

He appealed to the government to review its foreign policy in the Middle East, which has been unjust toward the Palestinians since 1948. Farrakhan also cautioned that the war on terrorism could usher in the Biblical "War of Armageddon" and called on Muslims (and perhaps others) "to pray" that innocent Muslims not be harmed inadvertently by American soldiers.

In his letter to President George W. Bush, dated December 1, 2001, Farrakhan identified himself, as usual, as the "National Representative of the Honorable Elijah Muhammad, whom I believe Allah (God) raised among the Black people of America to teach us Islam as a means of our reformation and resurrection." He expressed loyalty to America: "I appreciate the privilege that I have to live in America, and, with all her faults there is no nation on this earth where I would rather live." After cautioning the president not to kill the innocent in his pursuit of the guilty, Farrakhan offered to join a mixed-faith group to give the president religious advice. "I pray that we will be triumphant over terror and become the

Friend of Allah (God) in so doing," he wrote, and ended with the complimentary close, "I Am Your Servant in the war against evil . . ."

W. D. Mohammad has been known for his loyalty to the United States since his 1977 institutionalization of the New World Patriotism Day Parade held in Chicago on July 4. In February 1992, he opened a session of the United States Senate with Qur'anic recitation. Several post-September 11 issues of *Muslim Journal* reinforce his allegiance to his country and emphasize the duties and rights of citizens. Imam Mohammad bases his denunciation of the "terrorists" on Qur'anic verses, sayings attributed to the Prophet Muhammad, and widely accepted interpretations of those basic sources of Islam. He did not limit his condemnation of the attackers to their killing of innocent civilians. The destruction of the World Trade Center property was also un-Islamic.

Moreover, he compared the behavior of the "terrorists" to that of a "crazy animal"; they were "not in their good Muslim behavior" since their "extremist" acts were not in keeping with the Qur'an and the example of Muhammad: "They really are out of the circle and framework of Islam with their conduct. So we are talking about terrorists, not Muslims."

One of the most popular Muslim leaders, Imam Siraj Wahhaj of Masjid Al-Taqwa in Brooklyn, voiced similar sentiments regarding the incompatibility between the events of September 11 and Islam. Like other Muslim leaders, Imam Wahhaj supports a just American retaliation for the attacks, pursuit of the war against terrorism, and a balanced approach to the Israeli-Palestinian problem.

Thus, there do not appear to have been fundamental differences between the reactions of African-American organizations and those of the better-known associations led by immigrants—and apparently most international Islamic organizations. September 11 may well have produced an historic change in the general attitude of Muslim African-Americans toward government and improved relations between them and adherents of Christianity and Judaism. The change may be short lived. All African-Americans have always looked favorably on the principles of the United States Constitution. The problem has been implementation of its principles of justice, equality, and equal opportunity. Despite the hazards of interfaith cooperation, it could be helpful to further religious understanding—especially Christian understanding of Islam.

Despite increased efforts, the September 11 attacks have not contributed substantially to better relations between African-American Muslims and immigrant Muslims. If we understood each other and cooperated with each other, we could improve Islamic understanding and redeem the tarnished image of Islam in America.

Akbar Muhammad, Ph.D., is a professor of History and Africana Studies at the State University of New York, Binghamton.

PRISON AND THE STRUGGLE FOR DIGNITY

A FORMER CORRECTIONS OFFICER ON THE DEEP ISLAMIC ROOTS OF INCARCERATED AFRICAN-AMERICANS.

By F. Thaufeer al-Deen

For most of their history in America, Muslims who had encounters with the criminal justice system were for the most part African-Americans. But since the 1980s, more and more immigrant Muslims have entered the country, and the nature of the crimes for which Muslims have been arrested—burglary, assault, and narcotics—have changed to more exotic offenses, such as immigration violations.

Now, in the aftermath of September 11, Muslims in America have undergone something similar to the experiences of Japanese-Americans who were interned by the United States government during World War II. We've seen the establishment of the Office of Homeland Security and the passage of the Patriot Act—which allows for indefinite detention of noncitizens who are not terrorists on minor visa violations, allows more federal telephone and Internet surveillance by law enforcement, expands the ability of the government to conduct secret searches, gives the attorney general and the secretary of state power to designate domestic groups as terrorist organizations, and grants the FBI broad access to sensitive business records about individuals without having to show evidence of a crime. Both these developments result in policies that directly affect Muslims—invasions of privacy, ethnic profiling, and unexplained police investigations.

To understand the context of Muslims' fears about imprisonment, it's important to revisit earlier American-Muslim history. In the 1950s, American Muslims were primarily black and members of the Nation of Islam. Nation members had earlier been processed through a program of that organization called the "name assignment process." To acquire their new "name"—the famous X—the initiate had to write a letter to headquarters. Prison officials, in their mail inspection, encountered letters written in the Nation's stilted and mystical prose. Usually it was filled with anti-white hate language. While such mail reviews were normal to non-Muslims, for Nation members, the mail represented a communication link to their spiritual headquarters. The language of these prisoners contested the right of the criminal justice system to incarcerate them. Through the 1950s and 1960s, the ability of the Nation to send proselytizing lessons through the mail to its imprisoned members was a point of legal contention.

Eventually, however, in several court cases, some of them rising to the United States Supreme Court, Nation members won rights that had been previously denied other inmates. Over time, Nation members won the right to receive religious mail, the right to visitation by their clergy, the right to a nonpork diet, and the right to wear bow ties with their prison uniforms. Eventually, they also won the right, even inside maximum-security facilities, to have visits from their "ministers," and later to hold prayer services, meetings, and classes.

As a result of these victories, as well as their highly structured and disciplined character, members of the Nation set themselves apart from other inmates by prison officials. A love-hate relationships began to emerge over this time. Out of admiration grew a high degree of autonomy for Nation members, and, gradually, in a few facilities, the recognition by prison administrators that they could enhance control over inmates by enlisting Nation members as informants.

Later, in the 1970s, prisons began to encounter new types of Muslims. They tended to be orthodox Sunni and Shi'ite Muslims, and primarily immigrants. At first, members of this new group, owing to their smaller numbers, didn't participate in religious activities with earlier groups of African-American Muslims. But as the new group's numbers grew, they began to demand access to prison services and facilities. At the same time, they had no understanding of African-Americans' history in penal institutions.

One of the results of this lack of understanding is continued strained relations between African-American and immigrant Muslims. It's clear that Islam has always been "other" in the American penal system, which is rooted in a Christian view of criminal justice. For instance, crime is represented as "the fall" of an individual. The litigation process involves swearing on a religious text—the Bible. In addition, prisons tend to be located in rural areas, where encounters between visiting imams and Muslim prisoner family members and the rural prison employees have intensified Islam's "otherness."

In the post-September 11 era, conservatism grips the American government. In this new period, there have been drastic changes in United States criminal justice. Incarcerated Muslims are aware of these changes because of the degree to which they are seen as "the enemy" at the point of arrest. Nearly every "fact" and myth they have heard about Muslims confirm their status as "towel heads" and "camel jockeys." In local lockups, anecdotal evidence shows, the spiritual needs of Muslims are rarely addressed. There is no Qur'an, no clean place for prayer, no *halal* (Islamically permissible) food, and, if a family member visits, the typical screening procedure is excessively intrusive of Muslim women.

All incarcerated Muslims, it seems, are now suspected of being terrorists. Every rebellious act or word, every struggle to cling to one's dignity becomes a cause for a reaction from the guards. The isolated Muslim inmate begins an existence, far from home, family, and culture, that begins to affect him psychologically and, eventually, physically. This can lead to problems perceived by guards as non-cooperation and troublemaking. And so, pressure builds for affiliation with the prison security officers, who may be able to facilitate, say, a *halal* diet, a clean towel to pray on, or a Qur'an. For detainees, one price of these valued things can be uttering, whether truthfully or not, a whispered name.

Sometimes detainees seek to affiliate themselves with an amenable inmate group, such as Muslim gangs. In the African-American Muslim groups, members are often required to make *bay'a* (a pledge of allegiance) to the group's inmate leader. That leader may or may not be loyal to the group's external "free-world" leader. It is not a pledge to be taken lightly.

From within this safety net, Muslim inmates do their time. There is always the daily intrigue of imprisoned living—the power plays, "loves," and deaths, the pathologies of some of the correctional officers. Loyalty and the need for safety can be used as levers to press an inmate to serve and satisfy the needs and interests of others. For instance, prisoners serving life sentences without the opportunity for parole often "select" a prisoner with a shorter sentence as a "lifemate." To ensure that the selected "mate" is around longer than sentenced, the interested prisoner frames him and causes him to be convicted of some offense that adds years to his sentence.

Because of this, family visits are critical. But the visits are bittersweet because imprisonment is to everyday living as time travel would be to those left on Earth. For the prisoner, rapid changes occur in the larger society as the prisoner waits. Eventually, families snatched apart can crumble and die. And when the prisoner is released, children are older, the wife is more hardened, capable, and independent. This is anathema to many immigrant Muslim marriages and culture.

The central values of Islam can mediate this effect on released Muslims, but for the majority of released offenders, the change is jarring. For those who have been detained under the War on Terrorism, incarceration often means lost positions, neighbors' suspicions, and pariah status. The question is whether these Muslim detainees will be able to return as productive and loyal citizens.

I believe we are now a nation ruled by emotion and whim, not by law. And this reality confronts the free as well as the detained and incarcerated immigrant Muslim. There is the hatred of Americans towards Muslims. There is also a war, now, that has placed ethnicity, religion, and geographic origins in question.

But there is something else. It is a Christian fundamentalism that takes literally the Bible's prophecy of a time when "every man's hands would be turned against the descendants of Ishmael, the first son of Prophet Abraham and his second 'wife' Hagar." Those descendants of Ishmael are Muslims.

For too many of their years here, the newer Muslims have lived apart from an American society that they view in conflicting ways. By faith they understand that the Islamic way of life is preferable to American hedonism—yet they need to stay within American cultural norms in order to function in America. To what example will these Muslims now turn to escape hatred, detention, imprisonment, alienation? Perhaps it will be the earlier example, an example about which they are only dimly aware—the example of African-American Muslims.

F. Thaufeer al-Deen, a freelance writer and author of Islamic mystery novels, has had a long career in law enforcement and corrections at the state and federal levels. He continues to work in social services and is president of Dawahnet, an organization that assists and educates Muslims as well as the larger community.

MUHAMMAD ALI: THE REASSURING FACE OF AMERICAN ISLAM

BELIEFNET'S SENIOR RELIGION PRODUCER ANALYZES THE MYSTIQUE OF THE CHAMP.

By Deborah Caldwell

When Muhammad Ali converted to Islam in a flamboyant, defiant moment nearly thirty-eight years ago, not many people were happy about it. His own father, Cassius Clay Sr., declared that Ali had been "conned." Perhaps a majority of Americans weren't even sure what a Muslim was. Ali's trainer, Angelo Dundee, said he thought it was "a piece of cloth."

And that was the nicest thing said about Ali's new faith. Most people were simply appalled. For Americans in the 1960s, *any* kind of Islam was suspect to mainstream America. And Ali had converted to the Nation of Islam, the black nationalist movement founded by Elijah Muhammad and embraced by Malcolm X. So he was not only a convert to a foreign-seeming religion—he'd also chosen what was at the time the most politically charged and scariest branch of Islam in America. Meanwhile, he essentially betrayed his friend Malcolm X by siding with Elijah Muhammad instead of Malcolm, who had been silenced by the Nation of Islam leader.

Of course, all these years later, the world is different. There

146

are now between 2 million and 6 million American Muslims, and
the vast majority of those who are American-born Muslims—between 500,000 and 1.5 million—are African-American converts,
making blacks a critical component of Islam in America. Ali is
today a traditional Sunni Muslim, having left the Nation of Islam
in 1975. So while he initially made Americans aware of Islam, his
greater contribution may be that he later gave mainstream Islam a
big boost.

Today, trembling with Parkinson's disease but still feisty, he
is a beloved American symbol. And perhaps, when Americans look
back on the last decades of the twentieth century, they will recognize that Ali had a significant impact on the development of Islam
in America.

As the first bona fide American celebrity to embrace the
faith, Ali was a hero to millions of Muslims here and around the
world. Many African-American Muslims were inspired to convert
to Islam because of Ali.

Now, post-September 11, he remains the most visible American Muslim celebrity. Shortly after the terrorist attacks, he went
to Ground Zero to proclaim: "I've been a Muslim for twenty
years. . . . People recognize me for being a boxer and a man of
truth. I wouldn't be here representing Islam if it were terrorist. . . .
Islam is peace." The movie about his life, *Ali*, garnered a Best Actor
nomination for Will Smith.

"He's the pivotal person in terms of mainstreaming Islam in
a nonpolitical way," says Imam Talib Abdur-Rashid, who leads the
Mosque of Islamic Brotherhood in Harlem, one of the nation's
most prominent, primarily African-American mosques.

"Here he is, so many years later, no longer physically able,
but really he's become this symbol of America," says Abdur-
Rashid, one of many Americans for whom Ali's conversion was
an inspiration.

When Abdur-Rashid converted to Islam in 1971 at age
twenty, he revered Ali as a great athlete and as an African-Amer-

ican leader. Only later did he discover how much Ali was already revered in other countries for his Muslim faith. While it's well-known that Ali is popular in the developing world, Westerners often underestimate how important his religion is to his appeal.

"When Ali would have a fight, it was headline news throughout the Muslim world," Abdur-Rashid recalls. "I used to have a few copies of clippings from *al-Ahram* newspaper in Egypt. He was a tremendously popular person. Because we in the United States tend not to be connected to other parts of the world, I think that wasn't understood about Ali."

In the mid-1960s, in the early years of Ali's conversion, Abdur-Rashid was a teenage boy, still an acolyte and Sunday school teacher at a Lutheran church in Harlem. He remembers reading newspaper stories about Ali—most of them negative, he says—and listening to grown-ups in the neighborhood talk about this young black boxer.

"Back in those days you could turn on the television and see Ali fight, and it wouldn't cost you anything. There was no pay-per-view. Ali's fights were always televised on *Wide World of Sports* on Saturdays with Howard Cosell," Abdur-Rashid remembers. "Early in 1967, I happened to be home one particular Saturday, and I was looking through a newspaper. I noticed Muhammad Ali was having a fight. I turned it on out of curiosity, and I was flabbergasted by what I saw. This is the guy the newspapers were saying really can't fight? And I realized: they're lying. My next thought was that people who write in the newspaper actually tell lies. If they're lying about that, what else are they lying about? It was like a window opening in my mind that never closed. From that moment on, I was a rabid Ali fan."

Abdur-Rashid says the Ali movie, which ends at the moment of his 1974 win over George Foreman, with Ali's arms raised in victory, cuts away too soon. Abdur-Rashid remembers the ending with additional details: "When he sat down to talk to the press, he pulled out a copy of a *Muhammad Speaks* newspaper and he said,

'This victory is proof of the truth of what I stand for religiously.'

"He always kept that projection out there," Abdur-Rashid says, laughing.

The next year, Elijah Muhammad died. His son Imam W. Deen Mohammad led his followers into traditional Islam, with Ali among them.

"When Ali, particularly, became an authentic Muslim and began to travel all over the world, all that did was magnify greatly his popularity among Muslims," Abdur-Rashid says.

Today, no one disputes that Ali is an American icon, an elder statesman, someone who is revered and beloved. But how important do Muslims believe he is to the development of their faith in this country?

"Extremely important," says Abdur-Rashid. "A lot of Americans turn on their TV sets these days and see this about 'Islam,' and that about 'Muslims'—and they don't have a human face to relate what they see and hear about Islam. But over the past thirty-five years, Muhammad Ali was that human face the average person in America came to know and associate with being a Muslim."

Deborah Caldwell, Beliefnet's senior religion producer, was a religion reporter for the Dallas Morning News, *winner of the Templeton Religion Reporter of the Year Award, and winner of a 2002 American Academy of Religion Award for Best In-Depth Reporting.*

MUSLIMS, CHRISTIANS, AND JEWS

Muslims in the United States have no choice but pluralism. Fortunately, it is built into their faith. Especially
with respect to Christianity and Judaism, Muslims have
strict instructions from the Qur'an to respect both religions. Obviously, in a modern context, this doesn't mean approving the politics of, say, Slobodan Milosevic or Ariel Sharon. Rather, it means
honoring the integrity of both religions and affirming their strong
relationship with Islam as valid expressions of prophetic
monotheism. And what about Hinduism? What about Native
Americans, for that matter? Kabir Helminski answers succinctly in
"Islam: A Broad Perspective on Other Faiths": "God has not
granted a spiritual monopoly to any one religion," drawing the
thought from a verse of the Qur'an.

Islam found support among Christians very early, when
Muhammad sent a remnant of his persecuted party to Abyssinia
for protection. There, a Christian king took them under his wing
and ensured their freedom. This protective role of one faith for another has powerful applications for Muslims in America today. Is
it just a coincidence that Islam can be practiced more fully in this
mostly Christian nation than in many so-called Muslim countries?

Islam, Judaism, and Christianity have common roots, Muslims believe, in an earlier "primordial religion," the Dîn al-Hanif.
Each of the three great monotheistic faiths may claim certain brag-

ging rights on which is the most pure—but that, after all, is only human. Again, Helminski comments, "Muslims may believe that their faith corresponds most truly to that 'first' religion, but this is not sufficient reason to deny that other religions offer an approach to God."

It is worth remembering that in its fourteen hundred years, Islam has sometimes had a rough ride among Christians. There have been instances of oppression under Muslim rule as well, but nothing quite equal to the Crusades, the Spanish Inquisition, and the North and Central European Holocaust. Here in the United States, American Muslims face the same degrading social currents that challenged Jews well into the 1960s: small-minded community racism and political indifference.

Today, it is hard to imagine prolonged friction arising on the Muslim side of the U.S.-Muslim equation. American Muslims have a long tradition of pluralism on which to draw. After all, the first successful experiment in European pluralism took place under Muslim rulers in medieval Spain. And when hundreds of thousand of Jews fled Spain after the fall of the emirate in 1492, who took them in? Not Germany, France, or England, but the Muslim people of Morocco, Tunisia, Libya, Bosnia, and Turkey. Even Christians in the New World have sometimes benefited. When, for example, Roman Catholics were being persecuted by British Puritans in New England in the 1600s, a number fled to Muslim Istanbul, where the Ottoman government granted them asylum.

Today, American Muslims, with their racially integrated mosques, abstention from alcohol, and emphasis on family and community service, may contribute significantly to American society at a time when our society faces enormous moral problems.

ISLAM: A BROAD PERSPECTIVE ON OTHER FAITHS

A SUFI POET AND SCHOLAR FINDS RELIGIOUS PLURALISM NOT ONLY ACCEPTABLE BUT INHERENT IN ISLAM.

By Shaykh Kabir Helminski

My first encounter with Islam was not in a mosque, or through a book, but by meeting a Muslim. I don't mean a nominal Muslim, but someone who was actually in the "state" of *Islam*, which literally means the peace that comes from submission to God's will. I definitely was not looking for a "religion," but I was looking for what I imagined to be Truth or Reality, and I felt that Reality in the presence of this person. In a sense, you could say that Islam is not a formulation, an ethical system, a practice, or even a revelation as much as it is a relationship to the divine.

The five pillars of Islam—bearing witness that there is one Absolute Being, worship, fasting, charity, pilgrimage—are a means to establish that relationship and are common to all sacred traditions. But that essential, conscious relationship with a spiritual dimension is the heart of the matter.

So orient yourself to the primordial religion, the innate nature upon which Allah has created humanity, without altering Allah's creation. That is the authentic religion, but the great majority do not comprehend.

Turn in repentance to Him and remain conscious of Him: be constant in prayer and do not be among those who worship other than God, those who split apart the Religion and create sects—each group separately rejoicing in what it has! (Qur'an 30:30–32)

This verse suggests a broad perspective, as it refers to the timeless monotheism associated with the Prophet Abraham. This primordial religion corresponds to the human nature instilled by God. The purpose of religion, therefore, is to safeguard the human soul from "altering God's creation," from being less than human. It is possible, then, to make a distinction between that primordial religion or essential Islam, the authentic core of all revealed traditions, and the Islam practiced by the community of Muhammad, which is just one possible manifestation of humanity's primordial religion.

It is from the perspective of this primordial religion that pluralism must be accepted. Muslims may believe that their faith corresponds most truly to that "first" religion, but this is not sufficient reason to deny that other religions offer an approach to God. *For each one of you (several communities) We have appointed a Law and a Way of Life. If God had so willed, He would have made all of you one community, but He has not done so that He may test you in what He has given you; so compete in goodness. To God shall you all return and He will tell you (the Truth) about what you have been disputing.* (5:48)

This suggests that God has not granted a spiritual monopoly to any one religion. Competition in virtue reduces the chances that we will become complacent and lazy; competition in goodness increases the likelihood of humility and cooperation. *To every people have We appointed ways of worship which they observe. Therefore let them not dispute with thee, but bid them to thy Sustainer for thou art on the right way.* (22:67–69)

These ways of worship have been established by God Himself. Muhammad is not asked to convert people, but to establish a harmonious relationship with them by acknowledging one Sustainer. This verse in particular seems to guide the Prophet Muhammad to a cooperative relationship with other faiths. The Islamic worldview accepts other faiths, guaranteeing the right of other religious communities to follow their own revealed tradition. As the Qur'an says, "There shall be no coercion in religion."

RIGHTING THE MISUSE OF THE QUR'AN

Now let us turn to some verses of the Qur'an that have been misused by those who try to turn Islam into a narrow, exclusive belief system.

Indeed, with God the essential religion is submission, And it was only because of envy that the People of the Book developed other views, and only after knowledge had come to them, but whoever denies the signs of God, with God the reckoning is swift. (3:19)

Here we have one of the most important passages in the Qur'an, one that deserves careful reflection. Its context is a discussion of the essential elements of faith. The passage begins with a confirmation of the authenticity of books revealed to Moses and Jesus, referring specifically to the Torah and the Gospel. Within the context of this acknowledgement of religious pluralism, humankind is given a clear warning: "Those who reject the signs of God will suffer the severest penalty" (3:4). What does it mean to reject the signs of God? It is said that various things distract us from recognizing the signs of God: women and sons, heaps of gold and silver, fine horses (or nowadays cars), and real estate. Our *exclusive* preoccupation with the things of the world blinds us to the signs.

Submission, here, should therefore be understood as "islam" with a small "i"—a state of being, a kind of relationship with God—rather than the specific forms of religion we understand as "Islam" with a capital "I."

A friend of mine was visiting a Sufi lodge, or *tekkye*, in Bosnia. It was an enchanting location under an immense rock near a beautiful river. My friend asked a young man there how old the center was. "Two thousand years old," was the reply. "How could that be?" my friend asked. "We here in Bosnia have been practicing Islam even before the coming of the Prophet Muhammad," the boy replied.

Therefore, a verse like—*And whoso seeks a religion other than islam, it will not be accepted from him, and he will be at a loss in the Hereafter.* (3: 85)—needs to be understood in light of others such as the following: *We bestowed from on high the Torah, in which there is guidance and light. . . . If any fail to judge by what Allah has revealed, they are unbelievers* (kufâr). (5:44) In other words, Jews who follow the Torah are believers.

Finally, we have what may be considered a definitive statement on the subject in this verse: *Those who believe (Muslims), the Jews, the Christians, and the Sabaeans—whosoever believe in God and the Last Day and do good deeds, they shall have their reward from their Lord, shall have nothing to fear, nor shall they grieve.* (2:62)

Of course there are those who claim that this verse has been "abrogated" by verses like the previous one: *And whoso seeks a religion other than islam . . .* Nevertheless, Islamic commentators say that a verse can't be abrogated if it applies to a promise. Abrogation is permissible only with legal judgments, which may be altered because of changing times.

What principles of conduct and communication are proposed by the Qur'an in relation to people of other faiths? Without a doubt, it is an approach based on courtesy and gentleness: *And do not argue with the followers of earlier revelation otherwise than in a most kindly manner* (29:46; cf. 17:53; 16:125–28).

Even in the most extreme cases, where it is believed that people are following beliefs that are out of accord with reality: *But do not revile those whom they invoke instead of God, lest they revile God out of spite, and in ignorance: for We have made the deeds of every people seem fair to them. In time, they must return to their Lord, and then He will make them understand what they have done.* (6:108)

When the great Sufi Jalaluddin Rumi heard of two people arguing about religion, he said, "These people are involved in a very trivial affair. Instead of arguing which of their religions is best, they could be considering how far each of them are from the teachings of their own prophets."

It should be clear that Islam is in a unique position to act as a reconciling force among different faiths because Islam has built into its very nature the tolerance and respect for all religious communities and sacred traditions.

Furthermore, we are in a position to help realign these other communities with the original spirit of revelation. I can say that from my own experience, although I was raised as a Catholic, my affection for and understanding of Jesus only deepened through my Islamic perspective; I have heard others say the same. Islam can help them to understand the extent to which man-made beliefs have led to irrational theologies and self-serving institutions. We must safeguard our own religion from the same corruption. Anyone who thinks that these reflections contribute to a weakening of faith is, in my opinion, missing the point. It is precisely because of this perspective that I can call myself a Muslim. What is faith (or *iman*) if not the widest possible perspective on our lives, and what is disbelief or denial (*kufr*) if not a contraction upon our own narrow, egoistic concerns? It is because of this sweeping panorama of faith that I can take the Divine Revelation given to Muhammad into my heart and try to walk in his footsteps.

Kabir Helminski is a shaykh of the Mevlevi Order of Muslims (Sufi), which was founded by Rumi, and cofounder and codirector of the Threshold Society. He is the editor of The Rumi Collection, *a translator of several collections of Sufi writings, and the author of two books on Sufism,* Living Presence *and* The Knowing Heart.

JESUS THROUGH A MUSLIM LENS

MUSLIMS BELIEVE IN JESUS' MIRACLES. BUT THIS SHARED INTEREST
GOES MUCH FURTHER.

By Michael Wolfe

Jesus of Nazareth is the most widely revered religious figure in
the world. Not only is he central to Christianity, the world's
largest religion, he is also venerated throughout Islam, the second
largest faith.

Christians may be surprised to learn that Muslims believe in
the Virgin Birth and Jesus' miracles. But this shared interest in his
message goes much further.

In our scientific age, the miraculous side of Jesus' story has
greatly obscured his role in the prophetic tradition. In this sense,
there may be more important questions for Muslims and Christians than whether he walked on water or raised the dead.

In the Muslim view, Jesus' essential work was not to replicate
magic bread or to test our credulity, but to complement the le-
galism of the Torah with a leavening compassion rarely expressed
in the older testament. His actions and words introduce something
new to monotheism: They develop the merciful spirit of God's nature. Jesus confirmed the Torah, stressing the continuity of his lineage, but he also developed the importance of compassion and
self-purification as crucial links between learning the words of
God's message and possessing the wisdom to carry them out.

Oddly enough, some of the recent work by New Testament scholars seems to have reached a view of Christ not all that different from that of Muslims'. For us and for these scholars, Jesus appears not as a literal son of God in human form, but as an inspired human being, a teacher of wisdom with a talent for love drawn from an unbroken relationship to God. Both versions present him as a man who spoke to common people in universal terms.

AFFINITIES WITH JESUS

Two events in the life of the Prophet Muhammad may help explain why Muslims revere the Christian Jesus.

The first event involves an elder resident of Mecca named Waraqa bin Nawfal. This man was an early Arab Christian and an uncle of Muhammad's wife, Khadija. We know he could read Hebrew, that he was mystical by nature, and that he attended Khadija and Muhammad's wedding in about 595 C.E. Fifteen years later, a worried Khadija sought Waraqa out and brought her husband to him.

At the time, Muhammad was a forty-year-old respected family man. He attended this "family therapy" session in a rare state of agitation. He was frightened. He had been meditating one evening in a cave on the outskirts of town. There, while half-asleep, he had experienced something so disturbing that he feared he was possessed. A voice had spoken to him.

Waraqa listened to his story, which Muslims will recognize as a description of Muhammad's first encounter with the angel Gabriel. When it was finished, Waraqa assured him he was not possessed.

"What you have heard is the voice of the same spiritual messenger God sent to Moses. I wish I could be a young man when you become a prophet! I would like to be alive when your own people expel you."

"Will they expel me?" Muhammad asked.

"Yes," the old man said. "No one has ever brought his people the news you bring without meeting hostility. If I live to see the day, I will support you."

Christians will recognize in Waraqa's remarks an aphorism associated with Jesus: "A prophet is not without honor, save in his own country." But that a Christian should first have verified Muhammad's role as a prophet may come as a surprise.

The second important event concerning Islam and Christianity dates from 616 C.E., a few years after Muhammad began to preach publicly. This first attempt to reinstate the Abrahamic tradition in Mecca met (as Waraqa had warned) with violent opposition.

Perhaps the Meccans resented Muhammad's special claim. Perhaps his message of a single, invisible, ever-present God threatened the economy of their city. A month's ride south from the centers of power in Syria and Persia, poor remote Mecca depended on long-distance trade and on seasonal pilgrims who came there each year to honor hundreds of pagan idols, paying a tax to do so.

At any rate, Muhammad's disruptive suggestion that "God was One" and could be found anywhere did not sit well with the businessmen of Mecca.

Many new Muslims were being tortured. Their livelihoods were threatened, their families persecuted. As matters grew worse, in 616 Muhammad sent a small band of followers across the Red Sea to seek shelter in the Christian kingdom of Axum. There, he told them, they would find a just ruler, the Negus (king), who could protect them. The Muslims found the Negus in his palace, somewhere in the borderland between modern Ethiopia and Eritrea.

And protect them he did, after one Muslim recited to him some lines on the Virgin Mary from the Qur'an. The Negus wept at what he heard. Between Christians and Muslims, he said, he could not make out more difference than the thickness of a twig.

These two stories underscore the support Christians gave Muhammad in times of trial. The Qur'an distills the meaning from the drama:

Those who feel the most affection
For us (who put our faith in the Qur'an),
Are those that say, "We are Christians,"
For priests and monks live among them
Who are not arrogant. When they listen
To what We have shown Muhammad,
Their eyes brim over with tears
At the truth they find there . . .

Even today, when a Muslim mentions Jesus' name, you will hear it followed by the phrase "peace and blessings be upon him" because Muslims still revere him as a prophet.

We believe in God
And in what has been sent down to us,
What has been revealed to Abraham and Ishmael
And Isaac and Jacob and their offspring,
And what was given to Moses and to Jesus
And all the other prophets of the Lord.
We make no distinction among them.

As these lines from the Qur'an make clear, Muslims regard Jesus as one of the world's great teachers. He and his mentor John the Baptist stand in a lineage stretching back to the founder of ethical monotheism. Moreover, among Muslims, Jesus is a special type of prophet, a messenger empowered to communicate divinity not only in words but by miracles as well.

CONTRASTS WITH CHRISTIANS

Muslims, it must be said, part company with some Christians over the portrait of Jesus developed in the fourth and fifth centuries. Certain fictions, Muslims think, were added then. Three of these come in for special mention: First, Muslims consider monastic asceticism a latter-day innovation, not an original part of Jesus' way. Second, the New Testament suffers from deletions and embellishments added after Jesus' death by men who did not know him.

Third, the description of Jesus as God's son is considered by Muslims a later, blasphemous suggestion.

Muslims venerate Jesus as a divinely inspired human but never, ever as "the son of God." In the same vein, we treat the concept of the Trinity as a late footnote to Jesus' teachings, an unnecessary "mystery" introduced by the North African theologian Tertullian two centuries after Jesus' death. Nor do Muslims view his death as an act of atonement for mankind's sins. Rather, along with the early Christian theologian Pelagius, Islam rejects the doctrine of original sin, a notion argued into church doctrine by St. Augustine around the year 400 C.E.

It might almost be said that Islam holds a view of Jesus similar to some of the early apostolic versions condemned by the fourth-century Byzantine Church. Once Constantine installed Christianity as the Roman Empire's state religion, a rage for orthodoxy followed. The Councils of Nicaea (325), Tyre (335), Constantinople (381), Ephesus (431), and Chalcedon (451) were official, often brutal attempts to stamp out heterodox views of Jesus held by "heretical" theologians.

Rulings by these councils led to the persecution and deaths of tens of thousands of early Christians at the hands of more "orthodox" Christians who condemned them. Most disputes centered on divergent interpretations of the Trinity. For this reason, historians of religion sometimes see in these bloody divisions one of the root causes for early Islam's firmly unitarian outlook.

Then and now, no more dangerous religious mistake exists for a Muslim than dividing the Oneness of God by twos or threes.

Despite these important differences, however, the Qur'an repeatedly counsels Muslims not to dispute with other monotheists over matters of doctrine. People, it says, believe differently for good reasons. In fact, that is a part of Allah's will.

Beliefnet columnist Michael Wolfe is an American Muslim and author of One Thousand Roads to Mecca. *He is currently working on a documentary on the life and works of the Prophet Muhammad.*

WHY I LOVE
THE TEN COMMANDMENTS

MOSES HAS A PLACE OF HONOR IN ISLAM—AND ON MY VIDEO SHELF.

By Hesham A. Hassaballa, M.D.

One of my all-time favorite movies is *The Ten Commandments*, starring Charlton Heston. Although I am of Egyptian ancestry, I root for Moses and Israel throughout the entire movie. The depiction of the bondage under which the Children of Israel suffered pains me each time I watch the film. I'm riveted by the parts showing the Nile River turning to blood, the hailstorm of fire, and even the "night of death" when the first-born of Egypt die. But my absolute favorite part is the splitting of the Red Sea.

Surprised? Don't be. Moses plays a very prominent role in Islamic belief. He is considered one of the five mightiest Prophets of God along with Noah, Abraham, Jesus, and Muhammad. Moses is highly regarded in the Qur'an, where he is described as "the chosen of God" (7:144), "sincere" (19:51), and "honorable" (33:69). In addition, Moses is even more highly regarded because "God spoke directly" to him (4:164). There are more than 170 verses in the Qur'an that speak indirectly of Moses or mention him by name.

There are many stories about Moses in the Qur'an as well. The story of how Moses came to be raised in the house of Pharaoh

163

is mentioned twice. There are several passages that detail Moses' confrontation with Pharaoh after being commissioned to take the Children of Israel out of Egypt. In addition, the story of the golden calf (20:82–99), the parting of the Red Sea (2:50), and the Exodus out of Egypt (7:133–137) are all featured prominently. In fact, Muslims fast the tenth day of the first month in the Islamic calendar commemorating the Exodus out of Egypt.

Far from being prominent in the Qur'an only, Moses is also mentioned countless times in the traditions of the Prophet Muhammad. In one tradition, the Prophet rebuked one of his companions, saying, "Do not give me superiority over Moses" because all Prophets are equally honored in Islam.

Not only is Moses important in Muslim belief but he has also figured prominently in the shaping of the most important of all Muslim acts of worship: the daily prayer. According to Muslim belief, the Prophet Muhammad ascended to heaven from Jerusalem to meet with and talk to God. During this meeting, God commanded that Muslims pray fifty times daily. The Prophet Muhammad immediately accepted; it was Moses, however, out of compassion for Muhammad's followers, who insisted that Mohammed ask God to lessen the amount. Moses continually pressed Muhammad to ask God for a reduction until the number of prayers became five.

One cannot be a Muslim if he does not believe in, respect, and honor Moses. While the particulars of Muslim and Jewish belief may not be the same, Islam and Judaism still do have much in common, and the differences in our beliefs should not preclude our having a good relationship. I hope and pray that the common belief of the two faiths in Moses can serve as a much-needed bridge of understanding. It is also my hope that the common bond of Moses will help Jews and Muslims work together to finally end the bloodshed and bring peace to the Middle East.

Hesham A. Hassaballa, M.D., is a physician and writer. He is also director of the Islam in Public Action Committee based in suburban Chicago.

"MOM RAISED ME AS A ZIONIST"

A WRITER WHO HAS BROKEN BARRIERS HIMSELF CALLS FOR SPIRITUAL
BREAKTHROUGHS BETWEEN JEWS AND MUSLIMS.

By Mas'ood Cajee

My mom raised me as a Zionist. I'm not kidding. In fact, I made my
first Muslim friend only when I went to college. Let me explain.

As a second grader, I broke the color barrier at a white private school in Apartheid-era Johannesburg, South Africa. On the
first day of school, my mom gave me some motherly advice: Find
the smartest kid and befriend him. That smartest kid happened to
be Marc Weinberg, a Jewish bloke with brown hair and freckles
whose parents were involved in the Johannesburg theatre scene.

Marc and I even collaborated on a small stage production of
our own. We put on a play for our class that reenacted a battle in
the Crusades. I wrote a script, and Marc made costumes with his
dad's help. I think I played Salahuddin to Marc's Richard the Lion-
Hearted; we ended with a mock swordfight for Jerusalem. The
gentile kids loved it, even though our acting was atrocious, and we
hadn't completely memorized our badly written lines.

Soon, our mothers became friends. One day, Marc's mom
gave mine a manual on raising kids compiled by a South African
Zionist women's group. My mom claims she heeded the book's advice in raising me—and so I can claim that my mom raised me as
a Zionist.

No, she didn't teach me to sing "Hatikvah," and I can't read Hebrew, but I do like bagels and lox, I can pronounce "Hanukkah" correctly, and I once painted stage backdrops for a *Fiddler on the Roof* production.

More important, for my mother, the Zionist women's manual embodied Jewish values that Muslims in my family and community admired: an emphasis on education and the quest for learning, strong family ties, and community networks, mutual assistance, and discipline.

Muslims respected Jews for the way they helped each other, stuck together, got educated, and were paragons of success. Indeed, Muslims yearned for the day when our community could achieve the same.

At the same time, Muslims despised both the dark side of Zionism and the cozy relationship Israel had with the Apartheid regime. The same year Marc and I staged our play, Israel invaded Lebanon, seeking to crush the PLO. Ariel Sharon, who masterminded the invasion, was responsible for the massive bloodletting at Sabra and Shatilla, the Palestinian refugee camps outside Beirut.

In South Africa, unrest was growing in the townships. Stone-throwing black kids our age were being killed in the streets or detained and tortured. The guns used to kill them included Galil assault rifles, licensed to South Africa by Israel. Just as in the Occupied Territories today, the funerals for those killed became mass protests that resulted in more killing. Funerals thus came to sustain the unrest, as a new mass movement emerged out of cemeteries, community halls, churches, and mosques. Amazingly, the white students at the school I attended were oblivious to the rising tide of struggle against Apartheid. Marc and I spoke neither about the color divide that separated us under Apartheid nor about our religious identities. He knew that I was Muslim and nonwhite, and I knew that he was Jewish and white.

My mother, for her part, continued to raise me like a good Zionist Jewish mother.

When I was ten years old, my family immigrated to the United States. Following my mom's wisdom, I befriended the smartest kid again: a Jewish boy named Elie Finegold.

Once, I spent a Shabbat with Elie and his family. At the Friday dinner, Elie recited prayers in Hebrew, and we broke challah and had some good chow. We prayed for peace in the Middle East; Leon Klinghoffer had just been killed by Palestinian hijackers on the Achille Lauro. After dinner, all the Finegold kids put on a talent show. Elie and I did a hard-rock air-guitar version of "Twinkle Twinkle Little Star."

The next morning, I accompanied the Finegolds to the Shabbat service at the Herzl Ner Tamid synagogue in an affluent suburb of Seattle.

The rabbi spoke about Abraham and his two sons, Ishmael and Isaac. I don't know if the rabbi knew that a little Muslim boy was sitting in the temple pews that day, because he laid it out. There was a simple Biblical explanation to the conflict in the Middle East. The Arabs, descendents of Ishmael, were cursed and cunning. Being labeled cursed and cunning by the Torah is big stuff; you obviously can't have peace with such a people.

I think the Finegolds pretended not to hear what their rabbi was saying because we didn't bring it up afterward. I was unsettled and scarred, of course. I had an epiphany of sorts. I had been "othered" royally.

Since Ariel Sharon ignited the al-Aqsa intifada on September 28, 2000, Muslims attending their *jum'a* congregation prayers every Friday have also been subjected to the same vitriol from our imams and *khatībs* (preachers). The Jews are cursed; the Jews are cunning. No peace is possible when you base your very theology against it.

The Israelis, with their Bell AH-1 Cobra and McDonnell Douglas AH-64 Apache helicopter gunships firing Hughes Tow antitank missiles at Palestinians with stones and 1950s rifles, may have an overwhelming asymmetry in their weapons. But, judging from their rhetoric, rabbis and imams share an eerie symmetry in their pulpit demagoguery.

Breakthroughs on the spiritual and theological fronts by Muslims and Jews need to be achieved before peace can be had and violence quelled. Political handshakes and deals in the absence of serious spiritual dialogue and an earnest quest for justice will be meaningless.

Until a mode of peace and understanding between religious Jews and religious Muslims of all stripes can be brokered, peace will be no more substantive than a mirage in the Negev desert.

I know real peace is possible because I know that Muslims and Jews have lived together in peace for centuries before and because many of my own best memories of my childhood were spent with my Jewish friends.

Today, however, real peace will be attained only through atonement, reconciliation, and—above all—through the brave leadership and scholarship of wise and sincere Jews and Muslims.

Real peace will come, then, when the recognition of the dispossession of 1948, respect for the sacred geography of Jerusalem and other sites, and the right of return of the refugees are accepted and reconciled.

Real peace will come when the arrogant, demonic dimensions of Zionism and Palestinian nationalism are forever exorcised.

Real peace will come when the Qur'an and *hadith*, and the Torah and Talmud, become the blueprints of peace and coexistence that they are.

Until then, Israeli violence, Palestinian blood, a phony peace process, and sermons about the cursed and the cunning will prevail.

I know; I was raised as a Zionist. *Allahu 'alam.* And God knows best.

A dentist and writer, Mas'ood Cajee serves on the boards of the Fellowship of Reconciliation and Muslim Peace Fellowship. He lives in Cambridge, Massachusetts.

CULTURE

The power of the Word is not reserved exclusively to Muslim theologians and political observers. Ancient poets and modern stand-up comics have used it, too. It may surprise some Americans to hear that millions of unlettered Muslims around the world can quote long passages of the thirteenth century mystical poet Rumi. But how do they react when they learn that he is the best-selling poet in North America, too? Kabir Helminski tells more about this immortal versifier in his interview with Rhonda Roumani.

It's likewise an eye opener to read Daniel Abdal-Hayy Moore's account of his own evolution as a modern American poet and Muslim—over forty years. In tracing his roots through William Carlos Williams, Frank O'Hara, Allen Ginsberg, and other modern American poets, we have an opportunity to see how supremely adaptable Islam can be to modern literature and life. Yusuf Islam, the musician known as Cat Stevens before his conversion, has found new ways to adapt his talent—to help war-torn Bosnian Muslims, for example. "Education," he writes in "Islam Sings," "not simply entertainment—is still firmly the root of our media endeavors."

Culture is not exclusively about music and verse. In a novel discussion of where Muslim-American culture might go from here, stand-up comic Kamal al-Marayati explores the worth of cultivating a biting sense of humor.

Seventy-five years ago, the American poet Wallace Stevens remarked that

> *The whole race is a poet that writes down*
> *The eccentric propositions of its fate.*

As Islam takes root in America, her poets, writers, painters, musicians, and entertainers have unique experiences to explore. They will need all the precedents they can muster.

WHAT MAKES RUMI WHIRL?

A SUFI LEADER EXPLAINS THE APPEAL OF RUMI ACROSS FAITHS.

An Interview with Kabir Helminski by Rhonda Roumani

*Kabir Helminski is a shaykh of the Mevlevi Order of Muslims,
which traces its lineage back to Rumi, the thirteenth-century
Sufi mystic. Helminski is the translator of many books on
Rumi as well as several collections of Sufi writings. He has
toured the world, bringing the music of Sufism and the art of
the whirling dervishes of Turkey to people everywhere. He is the
author of two books on Sufism,* Living Presence *and* The
Knowing Heart, *and is the translator of Rumi's poetry collections, including* Jewels of Remembrance, Rumi: The Path of
Love, *and others.*

**What is it about Rumi's poetry that has made him so popular in
the United States?**

The United States is an openly religious country, unlike Europe,
where there is a lot more cynicism toward not only religion but
even toward spiritual matters. Americans are a naturally open-
hearted and spiritual people. Our spiritual history—the Euro-
Christian legacy—has been a legacy in which the direction of our
humanness and the direction of religion seem to be pointing in opposite directions.

And Rumi brings it back together by showing us that the way to God is through our humanness, through our brokenness. And only God dissolves our shame and helps us to know that we, God's creation, are profoundly loved.

Islam makes every aspect of human life sacred. Whereas there are other kinds of religious understanding that suggest the way to God is through the denial of our humanness and the overcoming of our humanness. The Islamic way is much more that we have an inherently good nature. We're not born with original sin. Muhammad showed a way to incorporate the highest spiritual attainment into a very human life. And this is frankly a pretty radical and new concept within the Euro-Christian tradition, where people have denied themselves and gone to monasteries and lived with the burden of sin.

Rumi speaks to this sense that we have of our own human limitations, our own human unworthiness, and he convinces us that we are loved by God. Through the embrace of our pain, a spiritual door opens *if* we embrace that pain in the remembrance of God.

So, Rumi is the voice of this unconditional love. He is willing to talk about his own pain, for instance—the pain of loving God, the pain of being human. He is honest. He touches our wound. He demonstrates how a human being can be the intimate friend of God.

Rumi was a Sufi. What is Sufism, and how is it connected to Islam?

Sufism is made up of several branches. We have no serious doctrinal differences between these branches, nor is one branch in competition with another.

Sufism comes from *tassawuf*, which means purification of the human heart without which we cannot know God. As the Qur'an says, "Indeed in the remembrance of God hearts find peace." The end of the training process of Sufism is the spiritually mature human being.

But we should understand that in every religious tradition, there are different levels. One level is the common practice of religion that they are typically born into. Within a religious tradition, there is also "the spiritual path" or "the way." The word for this in Islam is *tariqa*. *Tariqa* is a conscious choice that a person makes to go beyond belief to "experience." It is different than nominally belonging to a religion. In Islam, there are many *tariqas*. Someone who walks the path of *tariqa* is a Sufi.

In Islam, there is the level of *sharī'a*, or rules and regulations governing the lives of Muslims. The *sharī'a* governs our outer actions and behaviors. Sufism has more to do with the inner understanding of those outer practices and the quality of consciousness that we bring to those practices through the development of our inner spiritual capacity, particularly through consciousness and love. This development of one's spiritual capacity is much more possible through a relationship with someone who has made this spiritual journey and can help to guide us and help us avoid the pitfalls of the journey. This person is called a shaykh, a guide, a teacher, or sometimes just a spiritual friend.

It should involve a kind of apprenticeship. There are rare examples who receive this spiritual enlightenment without a guide, without a teacher. They are called *Uways*, after Uways al-Qarani, who Muhammad called the best of disciples.

How does traditional Islam look upon Sufism?

Sufis have had a place of respect throughout the history of traditional Islam. It has only been in relatively recent times, and through the confusion of modernity, that people within Islamic cultures have been denying the centrality of the Sufis. There have been a few times that Sufis have been on the outs—because of political reasons. But within the Mogul Empire, the Ottoman Empire, and throughout much of the Islamic world, the role of the *tariqa*s was respected, and people at the highest levels, even the *'ulama'*, or the religious scholars, were familiar and at ease with Sufism.

Many of the great Muslims have been Sufis: Abdul Qadir Jilani, Rabia, al-Ghazali, Rumi, as well as four of the five founders of the recognized *madh'hab*s, or schools of law.

But when you point this out, the critics might say, "Oh, that's not who we mean by Sufis. We mean those people who are lazy and don't follow the *shari'a* or those shaykhs who create cults around themselves and manipulate people."

For instance, when someone like Muhammad Iqbal, a popular Muslim writer and thinker, suggests that Sufis stand in the way of human progress, he is talking about a degenerated Sufism that may have existed in the India of his time. Iqbal described himself as a devoted student of Rumi and asked that a *makam* (or shrine) be built for him behind Rumi's tomb.

Imam Malik, a preeminent scholar of Islam and the originator of the Maliki school of thought, said, "To follow the *shari'a* without *tariqa* is to be a *zindiq* (misbeliever)." And vice versa.

Those who are critical of Sufism seem to view Islam as almost a contractual relationship with God. God has spelled out his part of the deal, and human beings had better fulfill it or they will be punished. But I do not believe that this was the mentality of Muhammad.

Sufism would be inconceivable without the Qur'an and the example of Muhammad. So those who tried to cut themselves off from Islam by ignoring the example of Muhammad and the revelation of the Qur'an have in fact cut themselves off from the source of Sufism.

Also, those who understand Sufism as the blending of all religious traditions into some new eclectic message are approaching Sufism superficially. The source of Sufism must be understood through a deeper understanding of the Qur'an and the character of Muhammad. And when one understands the Qur'an and the character of Muhammad, one will also have a compassionate and tolerant viewpoint of all faiths because that is the perspective of the Qur'an. But to create a spirituality by mixing a little bit of this and that tradition doesn't do justice to any of those paths. We can respect them—but we cannot walk them all.

How does Rumi's poetry fit into Islam? What order was he a part of?

Rumi's words are inconceivable without the revelation of the Qur'an and the example of Muhammad. Rumi received one lineage through his family and another through his teacher, Shams of Tabriz. These two lineages became the inspiration for a new lineage known as the Mevlevis, which for seven hundred years has attracted people with artistic and idealistic temperaments: musicians, composers, poets, calligraphers, and social reformers.

Rumi is not generally associated with Islam. Do people who read it in the West understand the Islam that underlies his poetry?

Rumi's writings fall into two basic categories. One category is the lyric poems—the *gazals* of Persia and *rubayat*. These poems are somewhat ecstatic and intoxicated. They don't often directly refer to Islamic teachings because they work in the language of metaphor and poetry. These poems also work in the conventions of classical Persian poetry, where people use the metaphors of wine and passionate love, knowing very well that they were referring to spiritual experiences and that these experiences are rooted within an Islamic context.

Nowadays, it has been these kind of poems that have been the more popular ones in America. Whereas his "Mathnawi," which has his more mature teachings and which contain references to Qur'anic *ayat* (verse) and *hadith* and Islamic practice on every page, is only now becoming popular.

Also, some of the most popular translations have had some

of the Islamic references removed because they would not be intelligible to the average American.

Rumi's message, however, is always about the love of God and the surrender to God. So even when he appears to be talking about passionate love or intoxicating wine—all of this is a metaphor for the surrender to God. And that quality of surrender appeals to people in America today, and they don't realize that this surrender is Islam.

Have many people come to Islam through Rumi?

Rumi's poetry is having an enormous effect in terms of softening people's hearts toward Islam. In America today, the reputation of Sufism among Americans is almost impeccable, whereas Islam inspires fear and prejudice. But for those who know about Sufism, and for those spiritual seekers or for those who have a broader consciousness, Sufism is universally appreciated and respected.

But most people don't know how to bring Islam and Sufism together because they find the Islam they are presented with or the stereotype of Islam frightening. Rumi and Sufism seem irreconcilable with Islam, but they are deeply related. In fact, most of the people who come to Islam come to it through Sufism. The only significant exception here is the African-American population, which came through another door. The vast majority of people in the West who come to Islam come to it through Sufism.

Are there Rumi sayings that have become popular in the mainstream?

For twenty years, I have watched permissions requests come into our office since we published some of the most popular Rumi translations, including those of Coleman Barks. There is something like a Top 10 Rumi quotes. The following would probably top the list:

> *Out beyond ideas of right doing and wrong doing,*
> *There is a field, I'll meet you there.*
> *When the soul lies down in that grass,*
> *even the words "you" and "I" do not exist.*

How do more traditional Muslims feel about the drinking references and the sexual imagery in Rumi's poems? What do they mean?

The Sufi literary tradition in the Persian language made use of these metaphors at a certain time to wake people up to the awesome reality of our possible relationship with God, which should be passionate and intoxicating. These great friends of God used these metaphors bravely, one could even say dangerously. It is interesting that even in Iran today, I have been told by very reliable sources, negative criticism of Rumi is unheard of, even though he wrote passages that were sometimes vulgar, though always to make a spiritual point. Today, there is more possibility for confusion in our own culture, where the metaphors are sometimes, relatively rarely, confused with their literal meaning. There is a book out called *The Love Poems of Rumi*. Well, Rumi never wrote "love poems" to anyone, except maybe to his wife—I hope he did. But he wrote many poems, one might say all of them, reminding us to love God.

Did Rumi whirl? What is whirling? And why is it done?

Yes. In Islam we're taught that *niya*, [declaration of] intention, is the foremost criterion of our actions. The intention behind whirling is to come close to God, to remove the veils, to come to our inmost center where we are closest to God. The whirling ceremony is one of the supreme aesthetic expressions, as well as a meditation in movement. But, most importantly, it is an act of worship.

Rhonda Roumani is the Islam producer for Beliefnet.

THE TONGUES OF POETS: SHAKESPEARE, WHITMAN, AND RUMI

A POET SEES THE QUR'AN AS A FERTILE SOURCE OF INSPIRATION FOR AMERICAN ARTISTS.

By Daniel Abdal-Hayy Moore

When I first became a Muslim in 1970 at the age of 30, in Berkeley, California, after achieving some small standing as a poet and creator of ritual theater, many of my peers were dumbfounded, disgusted or simply disinterested, fearing I'd veered off onto a wrong path and had landed myself in a backwater of spirituality, obedient to the dictates of a strange and suspicious religion, rather than the "Dawning of the New Age"—never mind that at the same moment I'd also entered a Sufi Tariqa based in Meknes, Morocco, where true ecstatics, visionaries, and wisdom-poets dwelt.

I believe I was perceived as having turned my back on the community of poets I had some personal acquaintance with, including Allen Ginsberg, Michael McClure, Lawrence Ferlinghetti and others—American poets of the post-war Renaissance, known universally for their vitality, directness, and spiritual aspirations, mostly Zen or Tantric Buddhist. Now some Muslims might categorize them as decadent, for one iniquity or another, but they represented to me the new searcher poets, non-academic, living life enthusiastically rather than vicariously—even seeking divine and total enlightenment—either *through*, or given voice *by*, the intensely fluid and immediate "projective" energies of poetry.

But when I discovered the Nicholson translation of the Mathnawi of Rumi, it made all my earlier poetic models seem almost arbitrary and frivolous. Rumi seemed to compose from the direct Presence of God, and in it I heard Allah's Compassionate Ocean, only a few ripples of which could be sensed in the American poets' works I had been, up to that point, so inspired by.

It wasn't until after I had become a Muslim/Sufi myself that I encountered the Qur'an, not a beloved text among the wild denizens of Berkeley's 60's, with its assertive do's and don't's. Immersing myself in its visionary flood, I realized that Rumi's work was really an elaborate and imaginative commentary on the Qur'an and Hadith, the life of the Prophet, his Companions and Islam's luminous saints, punctuated by long, delirious stretches of ecstatic gnostic flights. Only the Qur'an can be said to have been revealed directly from God onto the heart of a human being, peace and blessings be upon him, and it's clearly not poetry in the sense of intentional composition, but lesser winds of divine inspiration (*wahiyy*) blow forever, wherever a heart is ready and open to receive them, engendering true poetry among us that is highly revelatory, though not the Revelation itself.

Later I met our Moroccan shaykh, Muhammad ibn al-Habib of Fez, whose *diwan*, or collection, of poems, sung to traditional classical and folk melodies, was also the result of inspiration from God rather than rational composition—poems of beauty, direct experience and spiritual instruction—poetry as remembrance and the heart's deep pleasure. His Diwan and the works of Rumi, Hafez, ibn al-Farid, Shaykh al-' Alalwi and others, nourished in me the ideal of the enlightened poet, who, through ego-obliteration, and by God's generous grace, lets flow divine truths in the charged and endlessly interpretable language of poetry.

Which brings us to today, and our need, after September 11, to reject the spiritually bankrupt "fundamentalist" Wahhabism so influential over the American Muslim community, and forge for ourselves a new vivacity of Islamic life within the parameters of what is permissible *(halal)*. The diverse fertility of American culture is such that a rich native art should bloom, an art at once unmistakably Islamic, yet bearing our own brand of almost naïve freshness and open experimentation. For many, Islam has matured, and with deep Islamic roots, growth may flourish even more magnificently.

There is the song lyric, which in the hands of some Muslim rappers has already shown success in veering from the repetitiveness of macho pride. In poetry itself, there is a vast array of forms, without trying to shoehorn our American idiom into traditional Arabic or Persian prosody. In my own primarily lyrical poetry, I've taken Blake's dictum "to see a world in a grain of sand and a heaven in a wildflower" as the basis for searching for the direct perception of God in everyday epiphanies, using the spontaneous prosody insisted on by the Beats. But the field is literally open: epics, mock-epics, satires, history-rich and multiple-languaged Poundian Cantos, Ginsbergian Howls of anger and cosmic rather than merely rhetorical righteousness, Emily Dickinsonian compact brevity and enigmaticalness, John Donneian wordplay and ironical mysticalness, Dylan Thomasesque surreal-lyrical excessiveness—formal verse in strict meter and rhyme, or "open field" free verse whose anchor is the soul of the poem rather than the body. Anything but the doggerel that has become a joke around our house, of the somehow sanctioned *"I am so good, I do the prayer/I am a Muslim everywhere"* variety. I lament the seeming situation of present-day Islam vis-a-vis art, that if it's mediocre it's OK, but if it takes itself seriously and perfects it, it's *haram* (forbidden).

And then there is authentically inspired and heart-charged metaphysical poetry, the poetry of longing and mystical union, however you wish to define it, always a bit *transgressive*, which, as our own native Islamic history lengthens, we shall have the way Whitman bloomed late on the American scene, at the cusp of ripeness, spiritual thirst and social crisis, which is certainly where we find ourselves today.

It is said there is a *hadith* of the Prophet, peace be upon him, which goes: "God has treasures beneath the Throne, the keys of which are the tongues of poets." While it is true that the indigenous roots of American literature are mostly Christian Puritan, we as Muslims can sing our most loving belief in the Creator and His Messenger and message in a way that is authentic, modern and American at the same time, and in no way betrays the true spirit of Islam. After all, at the root of all humankind's religious paths is an intense spiritual awareness capable of releasing the profoundest songs of our hearts.

You'll Sing a Song

You'll sing a song from somewhere out of your depths
and light will hit it and it'll be
a diamond brooch worn at the back of
Layla's head in a sunny glade

it'll be a drop of water hanging at the
tip of a leaf in a dark rainforest radiating diamond light

a deep chasm with a train trestle above it and an
old fashioned train chugging along
oblivious to all danger over a giant arc filled with blue smoke

when you open your heart to sing
the whole room becomes a single ear

or even no ear at all but more like a
sharp point say of a needle about to
enter a cloth to sew
a saintly sleeve to the main body of the divine garment

the exact tip of the needle the sound-receiver
for the entire universe made drunk in the
sudden echoing orbit of your song

Daniel Abdal-Hayy Moore has had three books of poetry published by City Lights. His latest book, The Blind Beekeeper, *was recently published by Jusoor/Syracuse University Press.*

ISLAM SINGS

THE MUSICIAN FORMERLY KNOWN AS CAT STEVENS EXPLAINS HOW
THE BOSNIAN WAR TRANSFORMED HIS VIEW OF MUSIC IN ISLAMIC CULTURE.

By Yusuf Islam

The genocide in Bosnia at the end of the twentieth century was a
turning point for Muslims in Europe: It exposed people worldwide
to the hitherto unknown treasure of Islamic European culture and
civilization that Bosnia represents. The television pictures of blond-
haired, blue-eyed Muslims, chanting *"Allahu Akbar"* (God is
greatest) and reciting the verses of the Qur'an amid the smoke and
fury of the war, brought a whole new perspective to the concept
and understanding of Islam for many who, like me, witnessed it.

One of the outcomes of this terrible event was the reevalu-
ation of my position toward music and its use in Islamic sociopolitical life. The issue—I realize now—is certainly not as cut and
dried as it seemed when first presented to me back in 1977, following my embracing of Islam.

It's interesting to note now how my formative years as a
Muslim were shaped by those I came into contact with. I remember coming out of the Prophet's mosque in Medina and
meeting a fellow convert from America. This black brother asked
me who I was and what I did for a living. I told him I was a singer;
he let me know immediately his position, "Oh! You'll have to give
up that—musical instruments are *haram* [forbidden]."

As a new Muslim, I decided to follow the safest course, which was to leave that which was doubtful or unclear. So I gave up singing and performing, to the alarm of many of my fans and fellow musicians, until I knew more.

That was a parting of the ways, marking the line between my past and my present. Following that decision, most of my available time was spent establishing charities and working to serve educational needs of Muslim children in the West. I only wrote a couple of children's poems during the next ten years: "A is for Allah" was one of the results when I did manage to put pen to paper.

A giant leap in discernment regarding my understanding of culture and Islam came in 1992: the Bosnian War. It was the greatest violation of human rights and resulted in the most shameful and sordid crime against European Muslims ever seen— at least in my lifetime. During this time, I remember receiving an urgent call from the head of one of the Islamic aid agencies working in Bosnia. The brother pleaded with me over the phone, "Do something for the children who are being killed here! Organize an international concert—use your talent." It was very emotional, and I immediately felt inspired and began work writing a song called "Mother, Father, Sister, Brother." I had also half-finished a poem called "The Little Ones," which I dedicated to the children of Sarajevo and Dunblane.

Something had changed with the event of the Bosnian War; our perception of reality had taken a mighty leap forward. We— especially Muslims—were now shown the score. These indigenous Europeans were being killed simply because they were Muslim. In fact, many of them had already adopted Western cultural values: There were mixed marriages, some of them even shared a cigarette and a glass of beer with their neighbors, but that didn't help them—because they still had Muslim names.

Early in 1995, I was invited to a London hotel to meet the new Bosnian foreign minister, Dr. Irfan Ljubijankic. Dr. Ljubijankic was one of the unsung heroes of the war; for most of the siege of Sarajevo, he had worked tirelessly as a doctor in the basement of a

makeshift hospital. With no proper light or heat, he helped attend
to thousands of injured patients, many of whom had suffered
blown-off limbs and shrapnel wounds. Now he was a minister for
the Bosnian government, and I was truly honored to meet him.

It seems Dr. Ljubijankic was also eager to meet me: Somehow,
my songs and recordings of the seventies had made an impact on
him during his early years as a student. During our meeting, he
played me a cassette of a song he had written, entitled "I Have No
Cannons That Roar." It was extremely moving. I remember him
placing it in my hand and saying something like, "Please use it if you
can for helping the cause." Not long after that, we heard the news:
Dr. Ljubijankic had been martyred, his helicopter shot down in a
missile attack above Bihac. My heart dropped.

The Bosnian cause had been made to look all but lost. I realized that we required a confidence boost; our spirit had taken a
beating, and we needed to reassert our faith and identity. One of
the things that lifted me greatly was listening to the cassettes
coming out of Bosnia at that time; these were rich and highly motivating songs or hymns (nashids), inspiring the Bosnian army and
nation with the religious spirit of sacrifice and selflessness. There
was a new generation of singers and writers, blending the beauti-
fully melodious sounds of the Balkans with the message of Islam.

Dr. Ljubijankic's cassette recording was still in my possession.
Soon it dawned on me: Here was a magnificently potent tool; we
simply had to use it. But what about the conventional Muslim ban
on musical instruments? Many of these recordings had orchestra-
tion and instrumental backing; even if I personally refuse to touch
them, how could I justify their use?

But looking again at the question of music in Islam, it became more clear that the issue was still highly debatable, particularly in circumstances of oppression and war. Without doubt in
today's world, to have no cultural strategy or alternative would
leave Muslims without any defense. Surely, I thought, the use of
certain musical instruments for the protection of the Islamic iden-

tity and culture of a nation is worthy of the same allowance as guns and rockets? It was, after all, the self-identification and culture of Bosnian Muslims and their Turkish influence (i.e., Islam) that had come under attack—not the Bosnian's military might.

A *hadith* (a traditional incident or saying of the Prophet) may be worth quoting here. The Prophet was entering Mecca to perform his *'umra* (small pilgrimage) with a group of unarmed Muslims; they were being closely watched by their adversaries and long-time persecutors, the Makkan polytheists. A companion of the Prophet, Abdullah bin Rawahah, was walking in front of him, reciting poetry against the disbelievers, when Umar stopped him and said, "O, ibn Rawahah! In the presence of the Messenger of God and in the Holy sanctuary of Allah, you are reciting poetry?" The Prophet said, "Leave him, o Umar. These couplets are more forceful than the showering of arrows upon them."[1]

Interestingly, it seems that one of the closest similarities to singing and music in the Qur'an comes with Islam's attitude to poetry. Toward the end of the Qur'anic chapter entitled "The Poets," God Most High says:

As for the Poets, the deviants follow them.
Hast thou not seen how they stray in every valley,
And how they say that which they do not?
Except such as believe and do good works,
and remember Allah much,
and vindicate themselves after they have been wronged . . . [2]

We can see from this reference that poetry was generally disapproved of. It particularly alludes to the common ailment that many poets suffer; that is, their inability to emulate the noble words and excellence of their poetry. There are, however, always exceptions to this general rule, as seen from the verse quoted.

From a juristic point of view—although in the collections of authentic *Ahadith* (sayings and traditions) the evidence against the creation of life-like images of animate beings is much stronger than the ban on musical instruments—scholars are almost unanimous in accommodating use of pictures and illustrations in books and publications for educational purposes, while disputing the general use of photographs and TV for commercial purposes.

The foregoing only underlines the need to approach the issue of songs and music in a broader and more flexible context, without necessarily falling outside the rules of *shari'a* (rules and regulations governing the lives of Muslims), according to the needs of time and circumstance and choosing what is best for the good of the community—*Istihsan.*

"The war in Bosnia and Herzegovina is not yet over, it has simply moved into a new phase," to quote the Head Mufti, chief religious scholar Mustafa Ceric. Today, the danger facing Muslims in Bosnia and many other countries is not directly military, it is cultural: satellite TV, the Internet, CDs, fashion, advertising, the worship and adoration of sports personalities, film stars, and so on. This doesn't necessarily only affect Muslims—everyone is adversely affected by the media moguls and their commercial empires. Many Christians and people of various denominations are also working to offset the negative impact on their beliefs and traditional values.

If we are to withstand the bombardment of music, art, and philosophy based on morally unhealthy trends, we need to develop a unique and positive approach to the use of the media and its methods. A group of us have therefore started to produce CDs and cassettes: "The Life of the Last Prophet," "I Have No Cannons That Roar, "Faith," *"Bismillah"* (In the Name of God), and "In Praise of the Last Prophet" are outcomes of our strategy and the projection of our Islamic cultural vision.

Education—not simply entertainment—is still firmly the root of our media endeavors, for Muslims as well as non-Muslims, *insha'Allah* (God willing). Personally, I will continue to stay away from the use of instruments on tracks that I record, using only background vocals and drums: The Prophet said, "The *halal* [lawful] is clear and the *haram* [unlawful] is clear." I humbly suggest, therefore, that if a person really cannot tell the difference between sex-driven, disco music and morally motivating devotional songs, which help people to improve their lives, then this may quite simply expose a lack of perceptiveness on their part. To stay away from the doubtful for them would be advisable, if not necessary—as it was for me at one time.

The Prophet Muhammad said, "There is no sin beyond *kufr* [disbelief]." Many people still have not had sufficient access to the message of peace and the universal belief in One God, which Islam holds uppermost. Music is not the most important issue for a person first learning about Islam.

Nevertheless, after establishing one's faith in the One Supreme God and after accepting the Prophethood of Muhammad, as well as giving spiritual contentment, Islam also gives a person certain absolute directives on how, why, what, when, and where, to do things in his or her daily life. Regarding a number of worldly matters, there is an area of flexibility and *fiqh*. This is particularly true in the case of "music," where the term itself covers a wide range of activities and has no direct Arabic equivalent.

Mountain of Light, the multimedia company we launched in the United Kingdom in 1995, is the result of a cooperative effort. It was established with the intention of arming Muslims with a desperately needed cultural defense in order to strengthen and protect ourselves as well as to make public the message of our *dīn* (faith or religion). We will watch its effect on people with interest, praying that it will open many hearts to the light of Islam and the harmony it brings to society and human civilization: And we pray to God Almighty for forgiveness for any mistakes made in connection with our work; may He pardon us and guide us to what is best—*amīn*.

SOURCES: [1]Al Tirmidhi; [2]Surah al Shu'ara' 26:221–27.

Yusuf Islam, the former rock musician known as Cat Stevens, became a Muslim in 1977. He lives in England, where he is a leader in Muslim education and humanitarian projects. His new recordings, released on his Mountain of Light label, concern Islam and include spoken and a cappella compositions.

YES, THERE IS SUCH A THING AS MUSLIM HUMOR

HUMOR AND PIETY ARE NOT MUTUALLY EXCLUSIVE, ACCORDING TO THIS MUSLIM FUNNY MAN.

By Kamal al-Marayati

Muslim humor? What? Now *that* is funny! Jokes . . . about Muslims??? Isn't that *HARAM*? Of course not. After all, we Muslims follow a prophet who not only smiled often, but one who laughed so heartily that his teeth showed. In our striving to make a difference in this world, we often forget that. Plus, in these difficult days, there isn't much to laugh about. But laughter might just be the remedy that we all need. The image most Muslims have about comedy is that it makes light of serious situations and consequently trivializes things. It is true, comedy does make light of situations, but if it's done right, it sheds light and perspective rather than trivializes. Even further, comedy brings wisdom in a way that straight commentary just can't do. I've seen it myself countless times, as I'm sure you have too. But when it comes to Muslims and comedy, we seem to be lacking something. We're afraid to laugh at ourselves.

When we cultivate the ability to laugh at ourselves, that also gives us a license to make ironic (and insightful) points about others. It's one of the most effective methods of communication and understanding. Through humor, people learn about you. In a way, you become more human. I think I know more about Jewish culture and Jewish people from watching *Seinfeld* than I have by reading any book on the topic. But how many people think it's funny that I found more than two seams on my *ihram* AFTER I performed Hajj (pilgrimage)? Or my dad buying ten cases of "*Islamic* vinegar?" "Huh? No, Baba, it's *balsamic!*"

So who am I? Why should you care what *I* think about Muslim humor? Well, for starters, I'm an *Iraqi*, my wife is Indo-*Paki*, and my son's name is *Zaki* (now say that five times really fast). I was born in Baghdad, reared in Phoenix, and now I live in Hollywood. I was your average high school class clown/drama geek. I lettered in speech, and I wanted to major in theater in college. And, like your average class clown/drama geek, I was "strongly encouraged" by my dad to do something more practical. So, I became an engineer, reluctantly. Yet, even while I was being "practical," the impractical (and unfulfilled) side of me sought out places to be creative. I auditioned for Community Theater and took acting courses and loved it. I even got a gig imitating Jerry Lewis in an ice show at a major theme park. I eventually wound my way to New York and received formal training at the Actors Studio. And now I'm an actor. An actor who happens to be an American Muslim—one of a small but growing number.

Though I love to make people laugh (some would say I "need" to make people laugh), I consider myself an actor rather than a comic. But at Muslim functions, I'm always asked to do some sort of stand-up routine. And, since Henry V's "Saint Crispin's Day" speech wouldn't go over too well at a Muslim fundraiser, I usually do a few impersonations, and they usually love it. At a youth camp, I once wrote and performed a skit called "Haram oooor Halal." It was a game show parody where the host would state a situation and the contestants would buzz in their answer whether it was "*haram*" or "*halal.*"

Q: A horse you are riding stops to drink from a trough that you know has alcohol in it. Haram oooor Halal?

A: Haram because, if the horse sweats, the alcohol might transfer to the rider.

Needless to say, the skit created some controversy. Some people thought I was making light of the *sunnah* (recorded actions and teachings) of the Prophet, but my intention was only to parody our own zeal and preoccupation with minutiae. Others failed to even get the jokes and approached me afterwards, concerned that they hadn't known about some of the sins and wanted to clarify the rules so they could be sure to stay clear of them. I couldn't believe it—talk about mired in the minutiae! Though I assured them that the skit was only a parody, something tells me there's a whole generation of kids out there secretly nervous about riding on drunk horses.

So my hope is that, one day, we (Americans in general, Muslims in particular) can say "no pork on my fork please" and it can be as funny and as part of our lexicon as saying "gefilte fish." I also think we need to start writing and telling stories from *our* perspective rather than letting others tell us and the rest of the world who we are. That's my hope . . . and it's also my goal as an American Muslim comedic actor, *insha'Allah* . . . *Insha'Allah* . . . (God willing). Incidentally, ever notice how often and how strategically we use that phrase—*insha'Allah*? "The dinner will be at 6:00, *insha'Allah*." "I will do my best, *insha'Allah*." When my sister-in-law was a kid, she thought *insha'Allah* meant "probably not." "Mom, can we go to Disneyland?" "*Insha'Allah*." "Mom, can I have a pony?" "*Insha'Allah*." (Now you can laugh).

Kamal al-Marayati is a professional actor living in Los Angeles, a member of the Screen Actors Guild, and a lifetime member of the Actors Studio.

PRACTICING VIBRANT
ISLAM IN AMERICA

The essays in this section focus on the practice of Islam in
America from two different angles: the development of
mosques and community centers, where Muslims gather to
pray and serve their needs; and the performance of certain rites
like pilgrimage and fasting, which help bring home Islam's essential meanings.

My own first exposure to Islam was in the very rural mountains of Morocco, where any day one might watch a single man or
woman step aside from their work for a few minutes to perform
the simple postures of the Muslim prayer. There is a saying of the
Prophet Muhammad that "the whole world is a mosque," and indeed a Muslim is free to pray anywhere, so long as the spot is clean
and one is facing in the direction of Mecca. It was this remarkable
portability that, among other things, made Islam attractive to me
in those days. Not yet being a Muslim myself, I had no idea of the
role a mosque plays in the life of most practicing Muslims, especially those who live in pluralist settings like North America. A
Muslim can find salvation without ever setting foot inside a
mosque, but it must be obvious, from the opening essays in this
section, that for many American Muslims the *practice* of Islam re-
volves around this institution.

The two high points of the Muslim year are the month-long
fast of Ramadan, during which Muslims neither eat nor drink from

dawn till dusk, and the annual pilgrimage to Mecca, which a few million people actually perform and which the rest of the global population marks with a feast and celebration. Ramadan is not just a matter of things you cannot do. It is actually a period full of activity: the entire Qur'an is read in sections throughout the month, special community prayers are performed each evening, giving to worthy causes increases many times during the period, and even in poor families fine meals are served in the evening hours to relieve the rigors of the day-long fast. The final five essays in this section combine to shed some light, for Muslims and for those of other faiths, on these two central holidays.

MOSQUES TAKE ROOT
IN AMERICAN SOIL

OVER THE LAST FEW DECADES, THOUSANDS OF MOSQUES
HAVE SPROUTED ACROSS AMERICA.

By Michael Wolfe

A few years ago in St. Louis, I met a married Muslim couple with
grown children. They had come to the States as college students
in the 1960s. Like a lot of American cities then, St. Louis had no
established mosque. Instead, the couple gathered with a handful
of other Muslims at one of their homes for the Friday "congregational" prayer. This seemed satisfactory enough, until one day they
came to a startling realization: If either one died tomorrow, there
would be no place in St. Louis where they could receive a Muslim
burial. They made telephone calls. Apparently, the nearest Muslim
cemetery lay halfway across the country, in Washington, D.C.

This was the situation, then, for thousands of Muslims scat-
tered throughout America. I have heard similar stories from the
founders, now gray around the ears, of major mosques in every
United States city, including Los Angeles, Chicago, Atlanta, Cincinnati, Dallas, and Milwaukee. No mosque, no school, no Muslim social services, no bookstores, no Muslim funeral home, and no
graveyard. Fifty years later, things have changed so much that their
own grandchildren don't believe these stories.

Although estimates differ, it seems safe to say that there are several thousand mosques in the United States today (from three thousand to six thousand, depending on who's counting). They serve communities of varying sizes from a few hundred to several thousand people, in many small towns and every major city. What is more, a Muslim entering one of these establishments, were he or she fresh from, say, Egypt or Morocco, would be amazed by the variety of services available.

The mosques of America have had to provide, in addition to floor space for prayer, the fabric of a community that Muslims in the traditional homelands of Islam take for granted. If practicing Islam means something more than carrying out the rites of the religion, then American Muslims practice it differently from other places in the world, and one of the chief ways they differ is in their multipurpose mosques.

When you step through the doors of almost any United States mosque, each with its needs and often its own language, you find Muslims from dozens of different countries around the world. And therein lies the challenge of mosque-building.

Many American mosques are not only houses of worship but also well-staffed community centers with elementary school classrooms, religious classes, language classes, day care centers, bookstores, libraries, and, yes, funeral departments. There are speakers venues, movie screens, interfaith events, and fund-raising dinners. By attending the weekend speakers' programs at any of dozens of American Islamic Centers, a visitor may learn more about the world beyond our shores than from a week of reading the *New York Times*.

Since September 11, American mosques and Islamic centers have experienced an enormous surge in interest about Islam. This led local leaders to open the doors of Muslim institutions day and night, inviting the public in to hear and see how Muslims pray and talk and walk and show concern. Concurrently, Muslims in surprising numbers began calling churches and showing up to pray with Christians and Jews and Sikhs and others, in an honest show of solidarity. Reports from Los Angeles, a city with one of the largest Muslim concentrations in the United States, indicate that by December 2001, more interfaith activities had taken place in the area than throughout the past five years. The same seems to be true around the nation.

In my backyard, in the Silicon Valley of northern California, the Sunday after September 11, I and two dozen other Muslims took up an invitation from a Roman Catholic neighbor to attend Mass at a convent in Santa Clara. For many of our little group, this was the first time we had set foot in a Catholic church. The cloistered nuns of the convent invited us into their visitors' anteroom after the service, and a good exchange ensued on topics ranging from St. Francis to Pakistan, where one of the Catholic congregants had passed some years working in a hospital.

Within six weeks, our small, impromptu group had acquired a name, Interfaith Interaction, and had increased its active membership enough to sponsor a dozen visits to churches and synagogues every weekend, where they conduct well-attended public events about Islam, its relation to other monotheistic faiths, and how Muslims themselves were dealing with the loss and suffering triggered by the events of September 11. By now, this group has held dozens of mosque "open houses" in their area and visited more than two hundred temples and churches. All this was long overdue and demonstrates how, through sincerity and effort, faithful people find ways to draw good from the horrific.

The most deeply spiritual and disciplined among us may be able to sustain their spiritual lives in isolation. But most of us need the help of institutions to support and goad us. Mosques are now beginning to play a similar role in America to churches and synagogues. The importance of this can't be overstated. A proliferation of mosques in America will not only benefit Muslims—helping us to adapt Islam to the special needs of our local communities—but it will be good for the country as a whole. These will become institutions not only of Muslim renewal but of American renewal.

Beliefnet columnist Michael Wolfe is an American Muslim and author of One Thousand Roads to Mecca. *He is currently working on a documentary on the life and works of the Prophet Muhammad.*

THE FIGHT FOR THE SOUL
OF ISLAM IN AMERICA

AN EDUCATOR REMINDS US THAT AMIDST THE COMPETING AGENDAS
OF SALAFIS, MODERNISTS, AND SUFIS, ISLAM IS A BALANCED WAY OF LIFE.

By Yahiya Emerick

If you're like me, you care about Islam becoming a permanent part
of the fabric of this nation. You don't want to be the last Muslim
in your family tree, and you're convinced that Islam would make
everyone around you much happier if they only gave it a try. Now
if you get around, like I do, you've been to a variety of mosques,
conferences, gatherings, and dinners. You probably also have seen
at least one copy of the several types of Muslim magazines that are
in circulation. You've probably also heard a lot of different types
of scholars speak and heard a lot of different theories and concepts
presented for how to live Islam. And if you've noticed, as I surely
have, there is quite a range in the opinion and presentation style.
Some conferences, magazines, or mosques make you love Islam
while others make you feel like grabbing your faith and running
away and hiding.

What of organizations? The same holds true. There are
countless Muslim groups operating in North America right now. So
many, in fact, that a lot of everyday Muslims don't know whom
they should support and so remain inactive. Part of the problem

fueling this tendency to inaction is that we often don't see the members of many of the organizations practicing or implementing any meaningful sense of Islamic brotherhood. The real issue is not that there are too many Islamic groups out there—hey, the more Islamic groups the merrier! Neither is the issue whether the groups adhere to Islamic standards because if you're a Muslim, you work for Allah regardless of how helpful the people around you are.

The real problem is that each group seems to teach something different or to present Islam in its own, narrow way to the exclusion of the rest of the community. They give us their interpretations of what the perfect Muslim does and then they ardently try to get everyone else to follow this interpretation. Other Islamic groups, who may lean in a different way, are then labeled "weak" Muslims, misguided, or even heretical. If you're interested in participating in the building of a healthy, self-perpetuating Islamic community in North America, then you probably look upon all this foolishness and sigh in sorrow. But if you're really an optimist, as Islam encourages you to be, then you don't just complain about something—you try to understand the problem and then work toward a solution. So how can we learn to cure this problem, and how can we know which direction for change we must take? To do that requires a little analysis.

LIVING ISLAM'S POTENTIAL IN AMERICA

First, we have to recognize that Islam in America is probably closer to the true teachings of the Prophet Muhammad than anywhere else at any other time in the last five hundred years. I'm not saying that Muslims are better believers today. I'm saying that the access to pure Islamic teachings and the ability to live them to their fullest moral and social potential is more pronounced in America than it has been for centuries in Iraq, Turkey, Saudi Arabia, Pakistan, Afghanistan, Nigeria, or anywhere else. The Muslim world: Forget about it. It's too bogged down in stupidity, corruption, na-

tionalism, and racism. The light of Islam has been put out in the
Muslim world and has been reborn in the heart of the supposedly
secular, faithless West. There is nothing you or I can do to improve
the Muslim world. Nothing. Just accept it and get over it. Even the
Prophet left Mecca when he saw no more change could come. In
the open and cosmopolitan society of Medina, the focus of the
Muslims was in building a solid community that could live in relative safety. We are in Meccan times today in the Muslim world.
Islam has emigrated to safer lands where it can work on regaining
its strength.

Think about it: Living in the West is the real test of a believer. You're living Islam in a place where there are no restrictions
against your worship. No one will prevent you from praying here,
no one will make you shave your beard or remove your *hijab*. (If
someone tries, you can take them to court!) No one will make you
eat pork or renounce your beliefs. No one will make you stare like
a wolf at a pretty girl. No one will make you take drugs or alcohol.
No one can make you lie, cheat, or steal. No one will make you
open a liquor store or accept interest money. No one will prevent
you from living near a mosque. America today is a place where
anything, including Islam, is allowed. The whole matter comes
down to you. It's you who will either grow in strength and mind-
fulness of God or sink into depravity. If a person accepts Islam, he
or she can develop to the fullest moral potential, even while sur-
rounded by temptation. The advantage for Muslims here is that no
one can legally oppose you, and you have access to the most accurate Islamic information, from books to audios and videos. And
you don't have stupid village traditions about wily jinns, evil eyes,
and palm reading to dilute your knowledge, as is the case in virtually all Muslim countries.

So now that we know that the Islamic potential is the
greatest here, what currents are going on among the Muslims of
North America, and what forces are tugging at them? To be blunt,
we have some Muslims trying to import the refuse of the Muslim
world into North American Islam. At the same time, we have

some converts here who are trying to blend the refuse of the West into Islam.

Think about that for a minute. In most of our mosques and conferences, over half of what you hear is overseas politics or mindless promotion of thousand-year-old sectarianism. Meanwhile, I'm sitting here watching the second generation out in the parking lot of the mosque blaring pop music from their cars and talking to the opposite sex while their parents are inside arguing about things that have been argued about forever. This sectarianism has no place in Islam in America, whether it's the Shi'ite/Sunni division or the fundamentalist/modernist clash.

A few years ago, I taught in an Islamic school in Michigan. Fully a third of the students came from Arab Shi'ite families. The other two-thirds were from Sunni Arab families with the odd Indo-Pak kid here and there. By themselves, these kids mixed with each other and thought they were all just Muslims. It was beautiful. The second year I was there, sectarianism reared its ugly head. Some of the parents objected to the fact that a "Shi'ite" was on the school board. Some of the "Shi'ite" parents objected to the "Sunni" orientation of the school and to the performance of the Eclipse prayer in a certain manner. You can well imagine the situation six months later. Most of the Shi'ite kids, at the behest of a few parents, formed themselves into a unified block, and some even refused to pray with the rest of the students. By the time it was all over, the Shi'ite families pulled their kids out and opened a school of their own, and the Sunni families rejoiced, even as their school was plunged into chaos and financial hardship from the exodus of so many tuition-paying families. The baggage of the Muslim world, brought by those who came here, disillusioned a whole lot of people—for nothing.

THE NATURE OF THE DIVIDE IN AMERICAN ISLAM
Beyond the Shi'ite/Sunni issue, however, there is a heated ideological debate going on in the majority Muslim community. It

threatens to destroy the vibrancy of the rising Muslim community and has the potential to create a wide, new gulf between Muslims as serious as the ones plaguing the Muslim world. This debate centers around three powerful forces. There are the Salafis, the Modernists, and the Sufis. Most Muslims don't adhere to any of these three groups and rather prefer to just live as good Muslims. But because the organizations, magazines, mosques, and centers are often controlled by one of these three groups, it's inevitable that the regular Muslim becomes embroiled in contentious issues and stupidity. We all know that Islam must adapt to this environment to survive. No, I don't mean that the teachings or beliefs of Islam must change. Islam must stay intact for it to be acceptable to Allah. Islam "adapted" to Malaysia, Pakistan, Morocco, Turkey, Bosnia, and Gambia. No one complains about that. So if Islam needs to do the same here, then instead of complaining that our kids love pizza and hate kabobs or can't identify our home country on a map, we must work to see how we can implement the Islamic lifestyle in America.

What the three opposing sides in the struggle for the future direction of Islam in America want is for Islam to adapt here in their specific ideological way. The Salafi-style Muslims, who are often Middle Easterners, have a conservative vision that is usually tied to Arab culture and politics. They shun everything modern or Western—unless it can be used to further their cause. It is admirable, of course, to be interested in the truth, but in their approach there is no life, no love, no spirituality.

The Modernists are the most potent of the Salafis' enemies. They are made up principally of settled Muslim immigrants. The Modernists, who are often successful professionals, follow the Western-style secular-liberal tradition. In my experience, Modernists have three goals: assimilation of Islam into the American mainstream, promoting an interpretation of Islam that is loose and uncontroversial, and, curiously enough, the establishment of a class system based on status, position, and a well-defined hierarchy dominated by the leader class.

Once you give up the forms and structures of Islam, once you no longer really believe that it's true, then you defeat your original purpose, which is to stay intact as a community. If no one prays, goes to the mosque, or reads the Qur'an, then your community is reduced to iced-tea sippers who water their lawns on Friday afternoons. The paradox is that it's the modernists who make Americans less afraid of Islam, and they are also the ones who usually make the mainstream aware of our holidays and similarities with them.

The last group is the Sufis. The Sufis are a hard bunch to define because they run from one end of the spectrum to the other. There are "Popcorn" Sufis, usually white Americans who want to experiment with this mysterious and cool-sounding thing called Sufism. All they do is the chanting and dancing that they think is Sufism.

The legitimate Sufis are those who claim allegiance to Islam and who don't go overboard. Muslim Sufis in America are usually affiliated with mother organizations based in the Muslim world. They organize themselves into *tariqa*s, or orders, with a leader, known as a shaykh. Their primary goal is to develop love for Allah and to spread Islamic peace to other people. But in their emphasis on spirituality, they sometimes are as extreme as the Salafis.

While there is nothing un-Islamic about group prayer or molding one's self to model the Prophet's emphasis on love and understanding, many Muslims find that Sufis' style of dress (straight out of *Arabian Nights*) and their emphasis on tolerance at all costs can sometimes make their methodology difficult to model. In addition, many Muslims are put off by the term "Saints," which they apply to their ancient "Spiritual Masters." It has been noted by several contemporary writers that the Salafi approach has brought death to the faith of the second generation while the Sufi approach has caused faith to be reborn among the youth. If only we could take half a Salafi with his correctness and half a Sufi with his spirituality (and add a dash of Modernist adaptability) and put them together in one body, then we would have the perfect Muslim!

The Salafis drop out from spiritual draining, and the Modernists leave no second generation of believers behind them, and the Sufis drop away from too much fruitiness. Meanwhile, the masses of the Muslims are waiting for direction. How do these three trends interact in America? Basically, it comes down to the difference between spiritual content and legal exactness. The tragic thing is, the most vocal elements among the Sufis and Salafis go to extremes. The most radical Sufis began to incorporate Saint-worship, wine-drinking, dancing, and hokey mysticism, while the most radical Salafis began to suppress any expression of joy. In addition, their suppression of women's rights is well-known.

Most Sufis and Salafis do not go to the fullest extreme. I'm talking about the leadership, the official ideology, and the methods and practices of the loudest proponents of each pole. Where do we go for reliable Islamic teachings? How do I adapt Islam to America and make my neighbors understand me? This is the condition of the battle for the soul of Islam. My advice to you, my Muslim brothers and sisters, is to remember that Islam is a balanced way of life, so seek balance by learning Islam from your own reading of the Qur'an and *hadith*, and don't let your hearts be swayed by those pulling you to an extreme pole. Join with like-minded people locally and form your own study groups, social networks, and functions. Whatever your situation, let's get to work putting Islam into practice!

Yahiya Emerick is an American convert to Islam who has been involved in interfaith issues and education since 1990. He has authored fourteen books for adults and children and has been published in many magazines, including the Journal of Religion and Education. *He is the founder of Amirah Publishing, where the mission is to publish American-oriented Islamic literature.*

NAKED AND VULNERABLE ON RAMADAN

A POET AND MYSTIC PULLS BACK THE NUMBING VEIL OF HABIT
AND OPENS UP NEW SPIRITUAL POSSIBILITIES.

By Shaykh Kabir Helminski

*"I pass the night with my Lord: He gives me food and drink.
Hunger is God's food whereby He revives the bodies
of the sincere ones (siddiqs). In hunger God's nourishment
reaches them."*
—The Prophet Muhammad

As someone who started down the path of Islam in my early thir-
ties, my first Ramadan fast was an experience for which I was
hardly prepared. Unlike those reared in Islamic households, I was
more or less bereft of the community support and the personal
self-discipline to enter the fast gracefully.

Physical hunger was only a part of this new experience. For
a while, I found myself like an armadillo out of its shell: unpro-
tected, emotionally naked, and vulnerable. The spiritual dimension
of the fast far exceeded any expectations I had. I experienced a
new sensitivity and tenderness. People I knew who were going
through the same experience reported similar feelings.

The first year was the hardest. I needed to unload a lot of

emotional refuse. In a conversation with a friend who had recently stopped drinking alcohol, I could see certain similarities. Alcoholics are often said to be "self-medicating." When the numbing effects of habitual drinking are withdrawn, a whole range of repressed emotional experience surfaces. Could it be, I wondered, that food might have a numbing effect? Don't people also consume food to cover insecurities and anxieties?

Might it be that the fast of Ramadan was pulling back the numbing veil of my habitual consumption, exposing to me what lay beneath?

If this is true, then fasting is like going cold turkey. It also provides the opportunity once a year to process a lot of undigested emotions, thus purifying the heart. After all, the Prophet Muhammad said, "Excessive food numbs the heart."

When we fast, we expose ourselves to our own emotional state—and become more vulnerable and honest with ourselves. Ramadan, then, contributes to overall psychological health.

"Fasting is the bread of the prophets, the morsel of the saints," a teacher of mine used to say. Fasting is meditation of the body, just as meditation is fasting of the mind. Fasting helps the body purify itself of the toxins that accumulate through the impurities of food and incomplete digestion. Fasting, as long as it is not excessive, is based on a positive relationship with the body, for it eases the body's burdens. Indulgence—whether in food, intoxicants, or pleasures—is a form of cruelty toward the body because of the price the body must pay for our so-called pleasures.

Purification leaves the body, especially the nervous system, in a more responsive state. Hunger reduces the need for sleep and increases wakefulness.

Eating our fill hardens the heart, while hunger opens the heart and increases detachment from material concerns. We become more free of needs, qualified by God's name, the Self-Sustaining, al-Qayyum.

Fasting has been a catalyst for awakening in all sacred traditions. The great Sufi poet Rumi, for instance, reminds us, "What sweetness is hidden in the stomach's emptiness. We are like lutes, no less. If the sound-box is stuffed full, no resonance. If the brain and the belly are burning clean with fasting, every moment a new melody emerges from the fire."

Over time, I came to understand the gifts of the month of Ramadan. And I have also learned something about these gifts from friends.

In a gathering of American Muslims, I once posed the question, "What have you learned from fasting?" A father of three said, "Fasting develops my conscience because I fast in secret as well as in public." An artist told me, "During Ramadan, I feel transparent. My mind is clearer to reflect; my body feels light."

"It helps me to listen to something deeper. I discovered that there is an inner governing power within me. I have come to value listening to that, as difficult as it sometimes is," an investment analyst remarked.

A journalist said, "It teaches patience and unselfishness. In patiently enduring a deprivation, we become sensitized to the suffering of others and are therefore able to hear their need."

The essence of sacrifice (from the Latin "to make holy") is to give up, to put out of the present moment something good—and so to energize our love of God, to awaken the possibility of being more in touch with a spiritual reality.

Each year, I sense the Ramadan train approaching, and I realize it is once again time to take a ride. When I get on board, I find myself in the best company and well-provided for.

Kabir Helminski is a shaykh of the Mevlevi Order of Muslims (Sufi), which was founded by Rumi, and cofounder and codirector of the Threshold Society. He is the editor of The Rumi Collection, *a translator of several collections of Sufi writings, and the author of two books on Sufism,* Living Presence *and* The Knowing Heart.

THE REAL MECCA

AN AMERICAN MUSLIM RECOUNTS HIS FIRST *HAJJ*.
THE RITUAL OF PILGRIMAGE OFFERS SERENITY AND IDENTIFICATION
WITH ISLAM'S RICH HISTORY.

By Michael Wolfe

Mecca, the best-known Arabic word in English, is more than an advertising slogan, as in "tourist Mecca." Mecca is a modern mountain city of one million people in western Saudi Arabia. Because only Muslims go there, outsiders don't know much about it.

Yet once a year, for a few short weeks, Mecca attracts more visitors than almost any spot on Earth. I'm heading there this evening as the sun sets over the Red Sea, flying on a jumbo jet with hundreds of other pilgrims, on my way to perform the Hajj, or pilgrimage. Today, most visitors arrive by air. In other ways, however, this is a journey into the past. Mecca, the birthplace of Islam, is steeped in history and legend. We are going back into the past for a few days, to recover some of our own original spirit, by walking in the paths of Adam and Eve, Abraham and Hagar, and the millions of pilgrims who have come here before us.

Leaving the airport, our bus climbs treeless mountains for an hour. We're dressed in timeless-looking garments: the women in simple robes of black or white, the men reduced to two lengths of unstitched cotton. It's hard to tell a sweeper from a prince. We take a vow as we don these clothes to regard Mecca as a sanctuary and to treat other pilgrims gently, with respect.

We leave more than fashion at the border. In some indescribable way we leave ourselves.

As the bus winds through town, I'm sitting next to a Bosnian student named Ali. "Sure, you have to be careful," he says. "Yes, the crowds are enormous. But look more closely. It's not your normal crowd." A glance out the window confirms this. Streams of men and women from 125 nations fill the sidewalks and streets. Yet no one is pushing. Everyone is flowing—a slow crowd, a patient crowd. "You just have to get into the swim of it," he says. "The best place to do that is in the mosque."

Mecca's mosque is hard to miss. Its coliseum-size walls and bright, moon-rocket minarets tower above the streets from blocks away.

This vast temple complex can hold a million people. Most pilgrims arriving in Mecca come straight here. Even at midnight the mosque is in full swing. A hundred thousand people fill the ground floor colonnades. It takes me fifteen minutes to pass from the outer gates to the core of the complex, where a white marble floor gleams under stadium lighting like an ice rink. This part of the mosque is open to the stars.

Here, I join a ring of five thousand people surrounding a small, stone building draped in black: the Ka'ba, a windowless structure with simple lines that Muslims call God's first house of worship. The rest of the temple complex is a mere surrounding for this modest, ancient building. The Ka'ba marks the direction in which Muslims pray all their lives. Seeing it for the first time brings smiles and even tears to people's faces.

The human ring around the Ka'ba is moving counterclockwise in a circuit called the Turning, a special form of walking prayer. Around we go seven times at a stately pace, while the still point of the Ka'ba towers above us. The movement of so many people in one direction sets up a soft, pervasive whisper on the floor, of clothes brushing skin, of bare feet over marble. The Turning continues day and night, with every pilgrim making seven rounds. Viewed from above, the people and building form a single figure—of God's house at the center of their lives.

My turns complete, I descend a nearby stair to the well. It is cool and dim down here, with a pumping station and several hundred basins. This is the well without which Mecca would never have existed. (It is mentioned in the Biblical Book of Genesis.) Like everybody else, I take a sip, then return upstairs to the last rite of the evening: a ritual jog between two hills on the far side of the mosque. As I move along, I remember the sweet-tasting water. That's how it is in Mecca. You become a vessel into which timeless meanings are being poured.

A hundred thousand more people arrive each day. Mecca during Hajj season bulges at the seams. Ten thousand people will come from the United States alone. As the city swells, the streets become extensions of the mosque.

One night I walk past a settlement of West Africans camped under a freeway overpass. All over town, people are strolling, meeting, taking tea, and shopping. It is a traveler's paradise.

THE NEXT STAGE BEGINS: DAY ONE

On the eighth day of the month, the next stage of the pilgrimage begins. At sunrise, the whole population begins to leave town together, trooping five miles into the desert. We arrive to find a tent city on the sands. One hundred thousand attendants have been occupied for weeks setting up this and other canvas enclaves along the pilgrim route.

By evening the vast encampment bustles. I climb a hill for an overview. In the dark, the sands resemble a great harbor. Down there, bathed in lantern light, two million people have left their running water and solid walls for makeshift canvas dwellings in the desert. For the next few days we will lead a Bedouin existence, following a pilgrim route among the dunes on a trip designed to remind us that life is a journey.

In the morning, our loose procession snakes a few miles farther east to a sandy expanse called the Plain of Arafat. Here a second tent city has been erected, surrounding a craggy hill known as Mount Mercy. From this hill, the Prophet Muhammad delivered his last sermon. Today we surround Mount Mercy on all sides, camped in acres of quadrangles arranged by nation. A quarter-mile of Africa leads into a tract of Pakistan, giving way to an Indonesian district.

A brief congregational prayer at noon (imagine a small country bowing down simultaneously) precedes a short sermon from the hilltop. This is the spiritual apex of the Hajj. Devoid of pomp, light, or ceremony, the day-long Arafat vigil has few requirements. It is largely an internal experience, a day when pilgrims stand before their maker.

Throughout the camps, the mood is meditative. An Algerian elder squats in the shade of an ice truck, palms turned up in supplication. Across the way, a dozen Turkish women recite verses by the religious poet Jalaluddin Rumi while a baby naps beneath a green umbrella. Over the hum of the crowd, a chorus of men on the mount chants an ancient round: "I am here, Lord, I am here."

This sand plain is rich in historical fact and legend. Muslims from half a world away have been meeting here yearly without a break for fourteen centuries. You see traces of this in the architecture. You hear it in the stories. For example:

The curve of a low stone aqueduct skims the valley rim for miles. It was placed here more than a thousand years ago by Queen Zubayda, the wife of Harun er-Raschid, caliph of Baghdad. (Readers may recall Harun from the *Arabian Nights* stories.) The aqueduct is still in use today.

A half-mile down the plain, a large mosque and courtyard stand at the crossing of several modern roads. Its minarets, green in the twilight, mark the spot of the ancient Namira mosque, a working temple in Muhammad's lifetime.

Arafat marks the outer limit of the Hajj route. From here, the path loops back toward Mina Valley; pilgrims make the journey in two stages, pausing midway to overnight in a bowl of rocky hills called Muzdalifa. Super Bowl gridlock is mild compared to the Hajj's traffic jams. Half the pilgrims inch along in a hundred thousand trucks, buses, and cars. The distance—about three miles—may take three hours to cover.

Jubilant chanting fills the air as we move down a sandy grade into a riverbed. The banks of this dry channel are half a mile wide and packed with pilgrims. Stadium lighting along the way turns night to day and adds a theatrical glow. In about an hour, the Hajj has transformed itself from a meditative vigil into a sweeping, medieval pageant.

Where the riverbed ends, we pour across a lighted plain, settling into another broad encampment on the plain at Muzdalifa. This most ascetic of stops on the Pilgrim Way is also the calmest and most peaceful.

PILGRIM'S PROGRESS: DAY TWO

At midnight we learn the Mina road has been closed temporarily. There's a bottleneck up ahead. The way is clogged.

A tiny human dot dressed in two towels, I'm standing near a pot of peppered stew, about to order a plate from the grinning cook, when I feel a stranger's hand slip into mine. It is the soft hand of an ancient Indian woman in a shawl. Her forehead, a foot below my shoulder, looks burned from her day in the sun. She's lost in the crowd, I realize, and running out of willpower.

Lacking a shared language, we make do with signs. Then she lifts my hand and we set off through the crowds, walking together for perhaps ten minutes. Finally, I spot a kiosk marked "Missing Pilgrims." We go inside. The woman is asleep before I leave.

I wake on a mat under the stars at 2 A.M. The moon hangs low over the hills. On every crest, silhouetted pilgrims dot the skyline. I climb a stony path and join a Turkish family from Berlin. The father trains a flashlight on the ground. Now and then his son bends to pluck up a pebble, holding it to the moonlight. All over the valley, people are collecting tiny stones.

This strange, quiet scene is in preparation for the last Hajj rite. Tonight each pilgrim gathers forty-nine stones. In the morning we will carry them to Mina. There, in the next few days, at allotted times, we will throw them at a trio of pillars symbolizing Satan.

Gathering pebbles by moonlight? Stoning the Prince of Darkness? Yes, indeed. Scholars call it lapidation. In a symbolic act with a double thrust, the thrower of the stone both repulses temptation and casts it out. Hajj rules require that stones be tiny, "no bigger than a bean," for the point of the throw is symbolic, not to do harm

I wash my stones at a tap and, having no pockets, tie them into a corner of my towels. Three A.M. The road has reopened. The camps are stirring. The Hajj is moving on.

I reach Mina at sunrise, but the mile-long concrete causeway leading to the pillars is already choked with pilgrims. I'm as eager as the rest to perform this rite, but the crowds make me cautious. The causeway, a recent addition to the Hajj, is as wide as an eight-lane freeway. Halfway along, it is split into two levels, so that twice as many people may hurl their pebbles. There are no cars. Just the steady echo of innumerable tramping feet. Today our target is the largest pillar, a fifty-foot concrete cone. Its broad base rests on the ground floor. Its upper portion pierces the roadway overhead. It is nondescript, like the causeway itself. The devil needs no decoration.

This first "throw," with its press of people and raining stones, creates some of the most frenzied and cathartic moments of the Hajj. I wait on a stairway above, as the first rogue waves of enthusiasts roll toward their goal. At points, the crowd's impulsion can lift you off your feet. If you lose a shoe here, or drop your glasses, you don't even try to pick them up. Stopping, even pausing, is next

to impossible. Indeed, pilgrims have died here from being trampled. For all its futuristic roadways, modern transport, and majestic
mosques, the Hajj is not a theme park.

When the tide ebbs slightly, I join the crowd and move into
its center. It is dark in the lower level of its causeway. I catch sight
of the pillar, and then we are upon it. From fifteen feet away,
people are rocketing their tiny pebbles with expressions of glee
mixed with relief and exhaustion. Wrists snap. Eyes flash. Men and
women are cutting in front of each other to get a clear shot at the
giant cone. I'm near enough now to hear the soft "nick nick" of
thousands of pebbles bouncing, then falling to the ground. I complete my throws and follow the crowd's flow, spilling through an
archway to our right. A minute later we're back in the sandy
valley, blinking, sunstruck.

Two hours later, I'm standing on a tent-strewn, rocky hill
overlooking Mina. It is midafternoon. We have thrown our stones
and had a celebration. Now the camps are still.

This morning the Feast of Abraham began, marking the
formal completion of the Hajj. By now, every family has sacrificed
a lamb from the acres of animals fenced behind the hillsides. The
pilgrims are languorous. The meat they could not eat is already
being packaged for freezing and shipping to poor families abroad.
Like most Hajj rites, today's feast commemorates a timeless story:
in this case, the last-minute substitution of a sacrificial ram for
Abraham's son, an event regarded by Muslims, Jews, and Christians alike as an act of divine mercy.

AFTER THE FEAST

The desert march is over. Gazing down on this transitory scene, I
am reminded how the Hajj has changed its shape a dozen times.
A circle dance, a run march, a picnic on the dunes, a turning, a running, a vigil, a throwing, a feast, and a sacrifice have all led by turns
to a sense of completion that can't quite be expressed.

But the pilgrims try. Mecca boasts more phone booths than any place I've seen. Long lines of pilgrims stand waiting on every corner to call home, to report the good news, to be congratulated: The Hajj is over! We're back in town! We've made it! As the pilgrims' thoughts turn to home and loved ones, they embark on a shopping spree. From a street vendor's trinkets to the most expensive silks and diamonds, if the present comes from Mecca, it is special. The best gift of all is a jug of water from the Zamzam well. Mecca marks the heart of Islam; water is its essence. People back home will use it for special occasions only: a birth, a funeral, a marriage, saving even a small bottle for years.

Once the three-day feast concludes, tradition cautions pilgrims not to linger. As with any special place, staying too long may bring indifference. The idea is to leave Mecca before it leaves you. Jets depart daily by the hundreds; whole nations disappear before my eyes.

When my turn comes, I go down to the mosque again to say good-bye. This last Hajj requirement is called the Farewell Circuit, seven final turns around the Ka'ba. It looks serene, reflected in white marble. Leaving the mosque, I turn back to see it one last time. I catch a bus out of town. Soon we are gliding down the mountain highway, heading back to the airport, leaving behind the city that has called us from so many corners of the Earth.

Beliefnet columnist Michael Wolfe is an American Muslim and author of One Thousand Roads to Mecca. *He is currently working on a documentary on the life and works of the Prophet Muhammad.*

HAJJ IN A TIME OF WAR

DURING *HAJJ*, MUSLIMS ATONE FOR THEIR SINS—
BUT ALSO ASK GOD, "WHY US?"

An Interview with Moulana Ebrahim Moosa by Deborah Caldwell

Moulana Ebrahim Moosa, a professor at Duke University, is a fourth-generation South African of Indian roots who advised Nelson Mandela's government on Muslim issues. His criticism of authority that lacked "moral grounds" is believed to have prompted the 1998 bombing of his Cape Town home. Moosa believes Muslims must live in the modern world, in all its complexity. And that, he says, means painful discussions must happen before Muslims are comfortable with themselves. At the same time, he is also critical of America's foreign policy and of its moral and political culture, saying that the United States is in dire need of self-critique.

As we embark on the Hajj season in this time of war, what are Muslims thinking and feeling?

Well, first let's look at what Hajj means. Hajj symbolizes the fulfillment of pilgrimage, journey, struggle, and honoring the symbols of God. The pilgrimage is a way to honor those divine symbols. The Hajj culminates in sacrifice, according to the scripture. Abraham agreed to oblige God's will by agreeing to sacrifice his son, Ishmael. That represents his total devotion to God's will. And the Hajj represents the big test, the big trial in one's life. Abraham stands for one who has been tested over and over, so therefore, he's known in the tradition as a friend of God.

So pilgrimage in Islam is when friendship reaches a frenzy. People cry, they become emotional. Many of these people have suffered a loss of family, a loss of children, a loss of power. People come from countries where they've been hungry, where they've suffered. It's a highly emotional ritual, loaded with different layers. And you have three weeks of intense rituals.

So what would that mean for people going to Mecca during a time when global insecurity prevails? Muslims around the world are facing great insecurities. Muslim pilgrims will be asking God what has gone wrong. Why are we at the end of every stick? You have government brutality, repression in different parts of the Muslim world, political campaigns by people who do not hesitate to take lives. And there are bombs raining down in Afghanistan.

It's a very, very bewildering time.

What is the goal of the Hajj, and how will it relate to what's happening in the world now?

It does mean to reach a goal, to reach an objective. That objective is reconciliation with yourself and your creator. It's a moment of atoning. The pilgrim goes to atone for the past and to begin a new covenant with God.

For each pilgrim it will be different. Hajj becomes a very personal moment. Some people might be caught up in that one moment when they were rude to their parents. That will be the point that will make them humble. Or they will think about being saved from a tragedy.

But there will be the global concern. One thing they do become aware of is that Muslims feel in different parts of the world that they are under attack. And there will be nothing in the pilgrimage that will give them a solution. There will be no speeches that will give directives.

Yet they will try to put that aside to atone to God?

The atonement will be very, very personal stuff. It's about how one has conducted oneself in the past. People will be making commitments to be more observant believers.

But yes, there will also be a sense of bewilderment, a sense of disillusionment [because of what is happening in the world]. There's a very pessimistic sense, a sense of being trapped. Every voice I hear now talks of being trapped between a rock and a hard thing. There are no clear-cut pathways.

So the general pessimistic sense in the Muslim world will pervade Mecca, even as people try to keep it a personal spiritual journey?

Yes, because two groups seem to have "the answer" right now among Muslims: the bin Ladens and the people in the White House who are going to bomb everyone into submission. Hopefully, for the sake of the world, there are people who will not take those options.

In the 1980s, the Iranians tried to politicize the pilgrimage by holding demonstrations. They did it for a number of years, but then the Saudi government cracked down, and after that it stopped. These days the pilgrims are having random security done on them. And I worry that for people who come from remote Indian villages where they have never seen such things, for them this will seem like an intrusion, and something Western. And I worry that thousands of people will be further politicized as a result [against the West].

And in America, Muslims are at a stage of feeling despondency and pessimism. Depending on world events, that will be like a pendulum that switches. What is really required and will become necessary will be to do a lot of very, very hard questioning. The key issue will be questions of global social justice, in America in particular. The prophetic voice of religion in this country has not been heard.

We are caught in a cycle of patriotism, but when it runs its course I'm looking forward to the prophetic voice coming to the fore. There is a massive inequilibrium in global power. The poor are so desperate they'll do anything to fulfill their aspirations.

But during the Hajj, despite it all, I think that basically people will be looking for courage in the pilgrimage—and ways to strengthen themselves.

Deborah Caldwell, Beliefnet's senior religion producer, was a religion reporter for the Dallas Morning News, *winner of the Templeton Religion Reporter of the Year Award, and winner of a 2002 American Academy of Religion Award for Best In-Depth Reporting.*

HAVE QUR'AN, WILL TRAVEL

A YOUNG MECCAN WHO MAKES HIS LIVING CHANTING THE QUR'AN
CAPTURES THE ATTENTION OF "MODERN" MUSLIMS.

By Michael Wolfe

At a large and vivid party in a Muslim home in the Chicago sub-
urbs last spring, several dozen couples sat talking after dinner at a
long table.

Glancing around the room at thirty or more Muslims, I saw
a cross-section of American Islam in the new millennium: professors, doctors, business executives, teachers, housewives, therapists,
factory owners, and computer engineers. Some had been born in
Egypt, others in Lebanon, Palestine, Pakistan, and India. Most emigrated in the 1950s. They were forty-year Americans, part of a
global, centuries-old diaspora. The men wore business suits, the
women dresses; their children sported baseball caps and Nikes; and
everyone spoke English.

Then the table talk fell off and I glanced up. Down a long
hall, into the large room came a young, sandaled Arab wearing a
prayer cap and white flowing robes. Our host introduced him as a
Meccan, a young man from the heartland of Islam, whose livelihood lay in reciting the Qur'an. At his side stood a robed, bearded
elder from a local mosque—its imam, in fact, a religious scholar, a
man of respect, and a longtime Chicago resident by way of Cairo.

The two men settled into the only vacant spots at the table—two chairs across from mine.

We exchanged a few pleasantries—my Arabic is all but nonexistent, and the men in robes had between them about thirty words of English. We smiled a lot as the Arabic speakers among us tried to make our new arrivals comfortable.

A few minutes later, as the last of Islam's five daily prayers was called, melodious Arabic floated down the hall. Gradually, in the next five minutes, the whole party came to its feet and moved upstairs, reconvening in an upper room set aside as a prayer hall.

Fifteen minutes later, the prayer ended, our host stood again and told us more about the young visitor from Mecca: he was a *qurra*, a chanter of the Qur'an, Islam's sacred book.

The Qur'an is a work of such power and beauty that its rhythms, grammar, and vocabulary revolutionized the Arabic language the moment it appeared. Along with calligraphy, the reciting of this book has been the highest form of art in the Muslim world for more than a dozen centuries. And there before us, in the form of this young Meccan, stood a fine example of the grand tradition of Qur'anic recitation. Schools throughout the Islamic world continue to teach this complex skill, a feat of voice and memory, in dozens of different styles. To find the best practitioners, annual competitions are held around the globe, with a sort of World Cup Finals held in Brunei. There, the winner achieves world fame.

These days the truly great reciters cut boxed CD sets of the entire Qur'an. None are more prized than those recorded by the experts of Mecca and Medina, the holiest cities in Islam and centers of religious study for fourteen hundred years.

The young man before us had started early: at the age of five he had been apprenticed to masters of the field in Mecca, Medina, and then in Cairo. Fifteen years later, he began to travel, winning recitation prizes in Muslim cities around the world.

Someone at the party asked the young man to recite a passage. He rose, cupped his right hand to his ear, drew a short breath, and coasted into a faultless recitation of the ninety-first chapter of the Qur'an, called "The Sun." Everyone in the room was struck by his talent.

Consider the sun and its radiance, and the moon reflecting the sun.
Consider the day as it reveals the world,
and the night that veils it in darkness.
Consider the sky and its wonderful make-up,
the Earth and its expanse.
Consider the human self: how it is formed in keeping
with what it is meant to be,
And how it is imbued with moral failings
as well as awareness of God.
The one who helps this self to grow in a clean way
attains to happiness.
The one who buries it in darkness is really lost.

A reciter is not just a stylish voice but is considered a repository of the Qur'an, a sort of "human volume" of the book, if you will: because a *qurra* is not just a *qurra*, he is also *hafiz qur'an*: "knowledgeable of the Sacred Recitation." That is, *he has memorized the entire book* as well as the complex vocalizations of each syllable and word in the various traditional styles. It is simply astonishing to hear what Muslims regard as the word of God brought to such a perfect pitch of artistic concentration.

After the recitation, I discovered that the young man was looking for a job. In this, he was simply treading in the footsteps of generations of reciters before him. In medieval times, this same boy might be making the rounds of wealthy palaces from Cairo to Jerusalem to Baghdad and beyond, looking for a lucrative post as court chanter. Here in America, where pickings were somewhat slimmer, he was seeking work at a local mosque.

I have thought about him often since then. To an American like myself, his appearance in Chicago seemed somehow miraculous, representing as it does the continuation of a tradition that has been alive since the days of Muhammad.

But then, Islam's way of thriving in every region of the planet is itself a wonder. Historians have made much of medieval Islam as the first global trading culture. Just the other night, I came upon a Web site that, at the press of a few keys, delivered a full-screen live broadcast of the evening prayer at the Great Mosque in Mecca, complete with a crisp audio track of the Qur'an as it was being recited in the oldest mosque on Earth. These kinds of interconnections bespeak more than globalized trade and custom; they testify to the transportable nature of the human spirit.

I like to think the young reciter found a job, but I also hope that in the process he saw a good deal of this country: passing through St. Louis, Denver, Phoenix, Los Angeles, and coming to rest at last in some safe berth, but not before seeing for himself the extent to which his faith has taken root in a country with a democratic process, with an absence of kings or dictators, and with a constitution that protects religion from the state—a place where Islam has a real chance to flourish.

I hope he made it. I'm almost sure he did.

Beliefnet columnist Michael Wolfe is an American Muslim and author of One Thousand Roads to Mecca. *He is currently working on a documentary on the life and works of the Prophet Muhammad.*

WHY I LOVE BEING MUSLIM

In this final section, a number of well-known Muslims answer an all-too-frequent question: *Why would you want to be a Muslim?* Like Muhammad Ali in the early days of his own conversion, they speak at some risk to themselves, even today. It may be true that Islam is now tolerated *as a concept* in parts of American society, but as a personal preference, expressed in a public persona, it still can brand you. There are many reasons why American Muslims (a community numerically equal to the United States Jewish population) remain by comparison a shadow community. One reason is a natural aversion to being stereotyped and socially rejected in a climate that regards Islam with blanket suspicion. We include these remarks by famous Muslims not only because Muslims are proud of them, but because increasingly, it seems, many Americans can only be talked out of wild, erroneous social stereotypes by hearing famous figures puncture them on TV or in print. If Hakeem Olajuwon tells you that "God comes first" in Islam, you can believe it. If Mos Def confirms that Islam means serving others, it must be true. If Yusuf Islam, the singer formerly known as Cat Stevens, writes that Islam saved his life, then there must be something worthy about the religion.

This reminds us that, for all the puzzling reactions to its presence here, Islam, a faith shared by one in every five human beings, is not a religion forever rooted elsewhere. Rather, it is in America and here to stay.

I BELIEVE IN ALLAH AND AMERICA

AN AMERICAN LAW STUDENT WRITES OF HIS LOVE FOR HIS COUNTRY,
AND HIS CONVICTION THAT ISLAM BELONGS HERE.

By Arsalan Tariq Iftikhar

Myself included, there are over one billion humans on Earth who call God by his Arabic name, Allah. Out of that billion, perhaps five million of us call America our home. Many of us are born as Americans, study in American institutions, and go on to work and pay American dollars to our tax system. Like everyone else, we eventually find our better half, have chubby babies, go to zoos, get season tickets to the Chicago Bulls, go on our children's field trips, and fix the leak in our roofs. With all the growing pains in the life that we lead as normal Americans, every day we turn our face to Mecca to pray to what our Christian brothers call God, our Jewish sisters call Yahweh, and whom we call Allah.

Islam, Christianity, and Judaism have exactly the same origin. We each believe in the monotheistic deity of Abraham, who was the father of all three of these noble religions. Islam's moral and ethical standards are equivalent, if not more stringent, than those of modern day Christianity and Judaism. We, as Muslims, believe in every prophet of both Judaism and Christianity. We believe the world began with Adam and Eve and that the great prophets—

namely Moses, Aaron, Jacob, Joseph, and Jesus—were all divinely inspired by God.

We revere Jesus as a great prophet and the messiah of God. He is mentioned by name in the Qur'an thirty-three times. We equally revere the Virgin Mary as the mother of the Messiah. She is the only woman mentioned by name in the Qur'an and she is mentioned thirty-four times. Anyone who says Muslims don't respect women should read the entire chapter dedicated to Mary. How many times was our beloved Prophet Muhammad mentioned by name in the Qur'an? Five.

In Islam, a woman receives a monetary dowry from her husband, of which he has no legal claim. A woman is not obligated to change her maiden name. CNN happily broadcast women being oppressed by the Taliban regime. Islam abhors the oppression of women. The Taliban said women were not allowed to work, yet the Prophet Muhammad's wife, Khadija, was one of the most successful merchants in all of Arabia. Should we base our belief on a bunch of tribal warlords or the teachings of our Prophet?

In Islam, both men and women have to dress modestly. One aspect of this modest dress for women is *hijab* (head-covering). This is a religious mandate, but whether a woman decides to wear it is an issue between her and Allah because as the Qur'an categorically states, "There is no compulsion in religion." *Hijab* symbolizes empowerment, not oppression of women. It allows women to be judged on the content of their character, rather than their physical features that allow their objectification. When we see a nun covered from head to toe in her habit, we commend her on her devotion to God. But when we see a Muslim woman wearing *hijab*, she is oppressed. In how many likenesses of the Virgin Mary, sculptures or paintings, is her hair not covered? Not one. Was she oppressed? Hardly.

Muslim-American is not a paradox. As Muslim-Americans, we currently live in a diaspora, having to deal with an attack on our—yes, our—country. We also have a dual anxiety because our way of life, which is not far different from our Christian and Jewish counterparts, is under attack.

I am a law student. I study international human rights. I have been to U2, Sarah McLachlan, Dido, and OutKast concerts. I have been a ball boy for the Chicago Bulls. I have owned a Ford Mustang. I pray for peace and have read Dr. King's "I Have a Dream" speech ninety-six times. I may be a dreamer, but I promise you, I am not the only one.

I am a Muslim and I am an American. I am proud of both and will compromise neither.

Arsalan Tariq Iftikhar is the Midwest communications director for the Council on American-Islamic Relations, the nation's largest nonprofit Muslim advocacy and civil rights group. He is a native of Chicago and currently attends law school in St. Louis.

A BASKETBALL PLAYER FINDS PEACE

THE NBA GREAT TALKS ABOUT THE GIFT OF RAMADAN
AND CHANTING THE QUR'AN.

An Interview with Hakeem Olajuwon by Deborah Caldwell

One night in a Miami hotel room, Hakeem Olajuwon was pains-takingly reciting parts of the Qur'an—first listening to practice tapes, then repeating the Arabic scripture.

"I'm shy, but sometimes my voice is so clear and strong," he says. "Your tongue moves, and the Arabic language is so beautiful." The Qur'an talks to him, says the Houston Rockets center. From it, he learns to be pious and to stay close to God.

Olajuwon, thirty-seven, could not be a more devout Muslim. He carries a compass so he can pray toward Mecca from any bas-ketball arena. He reads the Qur'an on airplanes and visits mosques in cities where he plays. He gives 2.5 percent of his annual income to the poor and arranges his daily errands around prayer times.

"God comes first," says Olajuwon. "Paradise is not cheap."

And, as he has every year for the last decade, Olajuwon spends the Muslim holy month of Ramadan fasting from dawn till dusk, even as he plays professional basketball.

He awakens before dawn to eat precisely seven dates—the traditional Muslim fast-breaking food—and to drink a gallon of water. Then he prays for strength. He touches no food or liquid until sunset. Then he allows himself a well-balanced dinner—chicken, vegetables, and rice, perhaps.

When he plays an afternoon game, he pants for water—and drinks not a drop. Still, he says, "I find myself full of energy, explosive. And when I break the fast at sunset, the taste of water is so precious."

As difficult as the month seems to most people, Olajuwon says it is a gift. "You feel so privileged because this is a month of mercy, forgiveness, getting closer to God," he says softly, in a voice accented with West African cadences. "You do more good deeds in this month. You read more of the Qur'an. You study more."

In fact, he says, "You wait for it. You look forward to it."

The seven-foot-tall Olajuwon—one of Islam's most famous pop icons—has a well-known life story. The son of middle-class Nigerians, he grew up in Lagos and moved to the United States in 1980 to play basketball at the University of Houston. After helping the team reach the Final Four in 1982, 1983, and 1984, he signed with the Houston Rockets, which he helped lead to national championships in 1994 and 1995.

Olajuwon was immediately successful—but he wasn't entirely happy.

"I'm the kind of person who always wants more," he says. "I was successful materially, but I know life is much more than worldly success. I saw all these blessings God had given me. The way to give thanks is obedience to God."

Recalling his Muslim upbringing in Nigeria, he sought out a Houston mosque. Everything began to fall into place, he says, when he heard the Muslim call to prayer for the first time in the United States. "The sound of the call, when you hear the call to prayer, you get goose bumps all over," he says.

He began attending Qur'an study seminars and says he knew he needed to rededicate himself to his childhood faith.

In the midst of this rededication, he divorced his first wife—college sweetheart Lita Spencer, with whom he has a daughter,

Abisola, twelve. But in 1995, he married again, this time to Dalia Asafi. He has two daughters with Asafi—Rahma, three, and Aisha, fifteen months. He is rearing all three of his girls as Muslims.

Despite the culture shock of being a double minority in the United States—a black African and a Muslim—Olajuwon says he has found peace in his Islamic practice.

"Allah says in the Qur'an not to despise one another," he says. "So the criterion in Islam is not color or social status. It's who is most righteous. If I go to a mosque—and I'm a basketball player with money and prestige—if I go to a mosque and see an imam, I feel inferior. He's better than me. It's about knowledge."

While traveling during basketball season, he often taxis to local mosques for Friday prayer. Often, he says, worshipers there want to drive him back to his hotel. "It doesn't have to be because I'm a celebrity," he says. "People know that whoever gives me a ride gets a big reward from Allah. It's always for the sake of Allah."

In fact, he says, "If you do it for the reward, you get punished. If you get the opportunity to take a brother back to his hotel, that's a huge reward because you've done a good deed."

Olajuwon says he likes to talk about faith with his teammates, particularly devout Christians. Some of them, he says, "respond very well" to his polite—but persistent—efforts to convert them.

He says, for example, that when Christians talk about being "saved," they are describing a reliance on Jesus as "truth." But according to the Qur'an, he says, only Allah represents truth. And people who don't trust in Allah, he says, are living in what the Qur'an describes as "the house of a spider."

His conversations have led to some interesting exchanges. Once, a Christian teammate teased him for not eating pork. Olajuwon shot back, "If you followed your book, you would know you can't eat it either." (The Book of Leviticus proscribes eating pork, but that religious law is widely ignored by Christians.)

Another time, he got into an impassioned discussion of the

Christian doctrine of the Trinity with a teammate. First, Olajuwon says, his colleague said that Muslims "just don't understand the Trinity." But eventually, Olajuwon wore the man down to the point that he gave in, saying, "Nobody cares about it anyway." Olajuwon lets out a deep chuckle at the memory.

"If Christians follow the true teachings of Jesus, they come to Islam," he says. Muslims believe Jesus was a prophet—just like other prophets, such as Moses, Abraham, and Muhammad—who taught that people should submit solely to God, seek justice, and show compassion for each other.

Ever the evangelist, he is meanwhile anxious to spread Islam's truths to other Muslims.

"In the United States, I have an opportunity to interact with Muslims from different parts of the world," he says. "People bring new ideas from their own culture and background and try to introduce them as part of Islam." But usually, he says, when they actually study the Qur'an, they learn otherwise.

"Here, the information is more accessible" than in most Muslim countries, he says, because American Muslims tend to place a premium on understanding their faith rather than merely practicing a brand of cultural Islam from the Old Country.

Olajuwon even corrects his parents at times. An example: In Nigeria, older people are expected to perform a special month-long fast before Ramadan. "Not Islamic," he says. Another example: Forty days after someone's death, Nigerian Muslims slaughter a cow to celebrate and pray for the person. Again, he says, "Not Islamic."

For Olajuwon, Islam is a constant presence, not a straitjacket, but clearly a garment that binds him. He says there is "no negotiation" about praying five times a day. He washes his hands and mouth, turns toward Mecca, prostrates himself, and begins: "In the name of Allah, most gracious, most merciful. . . . You alone we worship. . . . Guide us along the straight path, the path of those you bestow your favor."

All day, every day, he says he has "God-consciousness," an internal voice that regulates his every action. "You don't forget for a second," he says. "There's a constant communication. You don't lose this consciousness. When I'm doing errands, doing whatever, I'm conscious of prayer times."

This God-consciousness follows him onto the basketball court. His religion teaches him to be merciful and kind. That means, he says, "You play competitively, but you don't do things that are cheating or unfair or foul play. You report to a higher authority."

Might he someday, after basketball, train to become an imam—and teach other Muslims? No, he says, quietly. "That's a big responsibility."

But Olajuwon says he might like to be a *da'i*, a kind of information broker who explains Islam to people.

"I'm doing it now," he says, laughing. "And what can be better than this?"

Deborah Caldwell, Beliefnet's senior religion producer, was a religion reporter for the Dallas Morning News, *winner of the Templeton Religion Reporter of the Year Award, and winner of a 2002 American Academy of Religion Award for Best In-Depth Reporting.*

MY ODYSSEY TO ISLAM

CONVERSION TO ISLAM OFFERS A MAN A WAY TO GET CONTROL OF HIS OWN SOUL.

By Steven Barboza

My abandonment of Roman Catholicism was spawned by the pre-mature death of my mother, at age forty-nine, on the day before my twenty-second birthday. I prayed like crazy for God to spare her, and when He did not, I established a new line of communica-tion. I called God Allah and prayed with my palms cupped (to catch blessings) and my eyes wide open (to keep Allah's creation in sight).

Given the irony and absurdity of events in racially torn Boston, where I lived, Islam was a godsend. A few months after my mother's death, whites assaulted a black man in front of Boston City Hall, using as a weapon a flagpole with an American flag at-tached. With that attack and my mother's death, a lifetime of frus-trations reached the breaking point.

My odyssey was not unlike that of hundreds of thousands of blacks in the United States. The journey became my jihad—liter-ally "struggle"—waged not for political power or economic en-franchisement but for control over my own soul.

Christianity did not offer a complete way of life to me the way Islam did. Attending mass once a week and calling it religion failed to satisfy my spiritual needs. Islam offered a code of conduct on how to run my daily life and how to communicate with God. Prostrating in prayer five times a day as a Muslim offered me more solace than I had ever found kneeling before a crucifix.

In 1974, as now, in the Roxburys and Harlems across America, only liquor stores outnumbered churches in vying for blacks' attention, and in my opinion, both stupefied millions of black Americans.

Islam, as I was familiar with it, seemed the perfect way to fight back. As a religion, it offered clear-cut guidelines for living; as a social movement, it stood for a pride born of culture and discipline.

Before my mom died, I had dipped into Malcolm X's autobiography. After she passed, I plunged into it. Malcolm had undergone a metamorphosis: from hoodlum to cleaned-up spokesman for the Nation of Islam and finally a convert to orthodox Islam, and through his own transformation he had shown that change, even from the most miserable beginnings, was possible.

Of course, Malcolm's life and mine were very different. He had discovered Islam in prison. I discovered it in college. He was the spokesman for a black theocratic visionary. I held down a mid-level white-collar job in a Fortune 500 company. Still, I felt a kinship with Malcolm and the Black Muslims. The color of our skin made us all cargo in a sinking ship, and Islam beckoned like a life preserver.

Two-and-a-half decades ago in Boston and New York, however, there were few orthodox mosques. In black neighborhoods, one institution, the Nation of Islam, dominated in the teaching of Islam, or, rather, a homegrown version of it. Many blacks who converted took to the Nation's teachings—its admonitions to self-love and racial solidarity, its belief in productivity and entrepreneurship. And with equal ardor, they also took to the Nation's other teachings—its racial chauvinism and belief that white people were genetically inferior, intrinsically evil "blue-eyed devils" who had been created to practice "tricknology" against blacks.

Using the twin motivators of myth and pride, Elijah
Muhammad built the Nation into one of the largest black economic and religious organizations Americans had seen. It claimed
a heavyweight boxing champion the whole world adored,
Muhammad Ali. Its women looked like angels in their veils, crisp
white jackets, and ankle-length skirts; its men cut no-nonsense yet
gallant figures in their smart dark suits and trademark bow ties.

But sitting in the Nation's Roxbury temple was like being on
a jury listening to a closing argument. The defendants (in ab-
sentia): white folks. The prosecutor: a dapper minister who practically spat, saying whites were so utterly devilish that their
religion was grotesquely symbolized by a "symbol of death and destruction"—the crucifix. The charge: perpetrating dastardly deeds
on blacks "in the name of Christianity." The verdict: guilty.

I barely lasted my one visit. To me, demonizing the "enemy"
as the Nation did hardly seemed the best way to learn to "love thy-
self." Anyway, I abhorred the idea of colorizing God or limiting
godly attributes to one race. And though Elijah deserved credit for
redeeming legions of blacks from dope and crime when all else, including Christianity, had failed them, I didn't believe that earned
him the title of Allah's "messenger."

So I moved to New York and became an orthodox Muslim
in the manner all converts do: I declared before Muslim witnesses
my belief in Allah and my faith that the Prophet Muhammad of
Arabia was his very last messenger. I entered a Sunni mosque and
prostrated myself on rugs beside people of all ethnicities.

Here was what I deemed a truer Islam—the orthodoxy to
which Malcolm had switched, the one most of Elijah's followers
opted for when the Nation of Islam waned after his death, the
Islam to which most of America's 135,000 annual converts, 80 to
90 percent of them black, belong.

On a plane to Senegal, I sat next to a black American
wearing a traditional Arab robe. The man was headed to meet an
imam, his spiritual leader, a black African Muslim. I later met other

black Americans who had spent years in Africa studying Islam. Through research, I found that up to 35 percent of enslaved blacks brought to the New World were Muslim. In converting, many black Americans may have been simply returning to the religion of their forefathers.

Over the years, I have come to understand what should have been obvious long ago—that Jesus had not forsaken my mother. She died because God had willed it, regardless of what form my prayers took. I hadn't rejected Christianity so much as embraced Islam.

Steven Barboza is the author of American Jihad: Islam After Malcolm X *and* The African American Book of Values.

"YOU'RE GONNA HAVE TO SERVE SOMEBODY"

RAPPER MOS DEF SAYS WE ALL DEVOTE OUR LIVES TO SOMETHING.
HE'S CHOSEN ALLAH.

By Ali Asadullah

Look at Mos Def and you see a poster child for the East Coast hip-hopper, Brooklyn division. But when he opens his mouth, whether plying his rhymes or just chatting, his eloquence shatters the preconceptions. What comes out is a surprising moral rectitude and religious focus.

"Black on Both Sides," his 1999 breakthrough album, has the same effect: witty title and a look that's all about street credibility. But the first words the listener hears are "*Bismillah al-Rahmān al-Rahīm*" ("In the name of God, the most gracious, the most merciful").

Islam has long played a prominent role in hip-hop. Among early rap groups like Afrika Bambaataa or mid-eighties groups like Poor Righteous Teachers and Big Daddy Kane, the Islamic inclinations were more implied than explicit. But by the nineties, Public Enemy was openly praising Nation of Islam leader Louis Farrakhan, and references to the 5 Percent Nation of Islam (a spin-off of the Nation of Islam) were popping up on albums by the Wu-Tang Clan and Busta Rhymes. Especially when the topic is social justice, an Islamic understanding has been a hallmark of socially conscious hip-hop.

Mos Def, however, represents arguably the first time that an artist, solidly wedded to the orthodoxy of the religion, has stepped into mainstream popularity with a complete, well-articulated Islamic message as part and parcel of that popularity.

Born Dante Smith in 1974, the Brooklyn, NY, native first learned the importance of Islam from his father, who was a member of the Nation of Islam before becoming an active member in the community of Imam W. Deen Mohammad (a son of Nation of Islam founder Elijah Muhammad) who brought the Nation of Islam into orthodoxy in 1976.

Raised by his mother in Brooklyn, across the river from his father's home in New Jersey, Mos didn't receive a formal introduction to Islam until adolescence. "I got my first exposure to Islam when I was thirteen," says Mos. "My dad taught me how to make *wudu'* [the ritual ablution Muslims perform before prayer]."

It wasn't for another six years, when he was nineteen, that he took his *shahada*, the Muslim declaration of faith. He'd gotten there by reading and personal reflection and after getting to know other Muslim rappers, like Ali Shaheed Muhammad and Q-Tip of the group A Tribe Called Quest.

Since then, Islam has been the cornerstone of Mos's life and of his socially and spiritually themed music. "You're not gonna get through life without being worshipful or devoted to something," says Mos. "You're either devoted to your job or to your desires. So the best way to spend your life is to try to be devoted to prayer, to Allah."

Tackling a broad swath of issues that include water rights, African-American self-esteem, and the destiny of humankind, Mos enlightens the listener as well as entertains. Taking on such issues, he says, is an Islamic mandate. "If Islam's sole interest is the welfare of mankind, then Islam is the strongest advocate of human rights anywhere on Earth," he says.

Mos puts special emphasis on the "anywhere." "It's about speaking out against oppression wherever you can," he continues. "If that's gonna be in Bosnia or Kosovo or Chechnya or places where Muslims are being persecuted; or if it's gonna be in Sierra Leone or Colombia—you know, if people's basic human rights are being abused and violated, then Islam has an interest in speaking out against it, because we're charged to be the leaders of humanity."

Mos's vehemence is somewhat rare in a hip-hop culture dominated by superficiality. Lyrics these days bet heavily on the financially successful triumvirate of sex, violence, and materialism. Mos credits his parents with guiding him away from such negative content. His father has been advising him on professional decisions for several years now. "My parents have been vocal and influential in all the decisions I made in my life," says Mos. "It made sense to me to include [my father] officially and to include my mother officially 'cause she'd been there from the beginning. You need to have that synergy—because who really cares the most about you?"

This family oriented approach is most evident in Mos's choices about his management. His mother, Sheron, and father, Abdul Rahman—whom he refers to affectionately as Umi and Abi—handle everything from media calls to general management and corporate strategy. Mos's brother tackles technical matters in the studio, and when it's time to hit the road, the entire clan travels together. "I just try to stay around the right people," says Mos. "I try to stay around family . . . [try] to stay around people who believe what I believe and [beg] Allah to help me."

His strategy has worked. After the critical acclaim for "Black on Both Sides," Mos was tapped by MTV for a recurring role on *The Lyricists Lounge Show*. He also appeared in Spike Lee's *Bamboozled*, ABC's *NYPD Blue*, and a Broadway play, *Topdog/Underdog*, which won a 2002 Pulitzer Prize. Nike gave its seal of approval by choosing his track "Umi Says" to score commercials launching Michael Jordan's Brand Jordan Nike division. "They just called and said, 'Mos, we'd like to use 'Umi Says,'" he says of the low-key negotiations. "That was it . . . I wasn't savvy in my presentation at all. It was very natural and plain.

"That's really just somebody in his organization or [Jordan] himself just really responding to the song," Mos says. The thirty-second spots featured Jordan and other athletic standouts such as NBA stars Ray Allen and Eddie Jones, New York Yankee Derek Jeter, and world champion boxer Roy Jones Jr.

In speaking with Nike representatives, Mos raised his concern about allegations of sweatshop conditions at some of Nike's overseas plants. "I voiced pretty early on that the corporation has a little bit of a shadow cast on it, on its character," says Mos. "And it was something that was very personal to me. And we made a verbal agreement that they would make a donation to some community-based organization of my choice, to at least say that they're giving something back."

Giving back to the community is a high priority for Mos. He performed at a benefit for breast cancer awareness in Lake Tahoe, California, and in Los Angeles at a benefit to support the legal defense fund of national Muslim leader and former Black Panther activist Imam Jamil al-Amin (formerly H. Rap Brown), who was convicted in a controversial murder trial.

Social activity is part of Mos's mission as a person—as a Muslim—of conscience. "I'm just trying to do the best I can with what it is I have and begging Allah to help me."

Ali Asadullah is a freelance journalist based in Cincinnati, Ohio.

ABOUT MICHAEL WOLFE

Michael Wolfe is a columnist for Beliefnet and the author of books of poetry, fiction, history, and travel, including *The Hadj: An American's Pilgrimage to Mecca* and *One Thousand Roads to Mecca*. In 1997, working with ABC-TV, he became the first American to broadcast live from Mecca. He has recently co-produced a PBS television documentary on the life of Muhammad. Wolfe, a Muslim, lives in California.

ABOUT BELIEFNET

Beliefnet (www.beliefnet.com) is the leading multifaith internet site and media company for religion, spirituality, and inspiration. In 2002, Beliefnet won the Webby Award for Best Spirituality Site and was a finalist for the National Magazine Award for General Excellence Online. *Taking Back Islam* is Beliefnet's third book in partnership with Rodale Inc.